PRAISE FOR *LEADER*

MW01087274

"After forgiving his son's killer, Azim Khamisa found purpose in promoting nonviolence and the importance of truth, empathy, compassion, forgiveness, love, service, and community. Certainly, a role model himself, here Azim profiles his own leadership role models—peacemakers all—whose diverse lives have exemplified these values. An inspiring read."

—Ken Blanchard, coauthor of *The New One Minute Manager* and *Servant Leadership in Action*

"I have been in the foster care system since age eight, and your story and ability to spread the idea of peace inspired me to take the appropriate steps towards success as a thirteen-year-old. Following your presentation seven years ago, my attitude towards the world no longer represented hatred but took me down a path of forgiveness. Forgiveness of my biological mother, whom I deemed responsible for my being in the foster care system, and forgiveness of the world, whom I held accountable for all of my young confusion and pain. Today as a senior, I am extremely appreciative of the message you have and continue to spread as it has not only changed my life seven years ago, but still influences my daily journey."

—Vanessa Brunetta, student, the Bishop School

"Once again, Azim Khamisa asks the hard questions and provides the reader with a method to think and re-think what is really important in his or her life. The concept of 'learning through and from the difficult times' takes away the sting of what is not working and paves the way for wonderful new understandings and adventures. Something for everyone."

— Rev. Dr. Stephen Albert, director of the World Interfaith Network and author of *The Interfaith Manual*

"In this book Azim Khamisa shares ten plus people who have greatly influenced him, and at the end of the book he allows us to explore our own role models and some of the lessons we have learned from them, the blessings they have given us, and the questions they inspire us to ask ourselves. As I went through this exercise, I realized that leadership development is life-long. It is not just about developing skills in a particular field but developing the social and spiritual connections and understanding that allows who we are and what we do to be a powerful influence for good in this world."

—Jan Chase, Unity Minister serving Unity Church of<br>Truth Pomona and leader in the Compassionate Pomona<br>Movement who is involved in Interfaith work

"Imagine joining a long-awaited family reunion with some of our most influential servant leaders, alive or deceased—including leaders of global communities, non-profit organizations and businesses, family leaders, and esteemed political and spiritual leaders. Imagine you could walk with each of them in nature and learn about their stories, their pivotal moments, and the competencies they've nurtured over time to lead for the greater good.

Azim's book is a special invitation to this precious gathering. These stories have touched my heart, expanded my mind, and gave me courage to act."

—Boris Diekmann, executive coach and bestsell-<br>ing author of "Chief Energy Officer"

"Leadership has never been more needed on our planet. Too many leaders are reactive short-term problem solvers. This book provides examples of unique leaders who lead not only by example but through dedication to higher principles which guided them in every aspect of their lives. We are all leaders whatever our position in life. We can be visionary leaders with greater impact by reading and sharing the examples provided in this wonderful book."

—William Gladstone, author of the international bestseller *The Twelve*

"Azim Khamisa eloquently makes the case for an updated brand of leadership that the world desperately needs—one focused not only on success metrics, but also on truth and compassion. Highly recommended both for those seeking formal leadership positions and anyone aspiring to grow as a person."

—Mark Gober, author of *An End to Upside Down Thinking*

"After years of dedication to developing his commitment to a deeper understanding of our personal and leadership journey in life, Azim has captured that wisdom through stories of inspirational leadership. Satyagrahi Leadership brings together the principles of truly impactful leadership through the experiences and lives of a diverse set of leaders. By reading these diverse stories, I found both connection and inspiration in them, regardless of their background or circumstances. Often, we see our ability to impact the world and those around us as a product of our environment and circumstances. These stories disprove that belief, and the leaders profiled, along with the impact they've made, shows us all that Leadership for the Greater Good is the path to truly leaving a legacy of making a difference in the world."

—James Hart, ret. CEO, Senn Delaney

"Who better to write about leadership than Azim, a true leader, who through tragedy, not only formed a foundation, so same fate does not befall other parents, but forgiving and having compassion for the killer of his son. It's been such an inspiring experience reading stories of other such leaders in his book."

—Azmina Jiwa, personal development coach
and author of *Freedom to be Me*

"In his new book, Azim Khamisa makes a powerful case for a new model of leadership that transcends mere career success in the service to a greater cause. Azim Khamisa has previously written about the compelling story of how the loss of his murdered son led him to forgiveness and ultimately to a deep sense of purpose and calling. Here the reader gets to discover a rich array of inspiring leaders who have been guiding hands on the author's journey, not in the least his own mother. It reminds us of the importance of role models, who I refer to as secure bases, to guide us. This book will definitely inspire you!"

—George A. Kohlrieser, PhD, Distinguished Professor of Leadership and Organizational Behavior, author of *Hostage at the Table: How Leaders Can Overcome Conflict, Influence Others* and *Raise Performance* and *Care to Dare: Unleashing Astonishing Potential Through Secure Base Leadership*

"Azim is an inspiration . . . he has faced one of the darkest experiences a human being can face and has transformed the suffering into love and forgiveness. He leads by example, and his message is powerful; his book is written from a highly conscious/evolved voice and is full of sound advice and inspiration to help us all step up as leaders and face the difficult issues of our times.

"We are indeed in a spiritual crisis, particularly in the Western world, where an overemphasis on capitalism has pushed this to the fringe, resulting in moral issues with potentially catastrophic results. Azim guides us all on how to recover this wisdom from Spirit, our only hope for resolving the issues at hand. He understands what Carl Jung was trying to teach us . . . that it is the whole person that creates whole societies, and only in whole societies can we live in peace and harmony.

"I highly recommend this book for all of us, as we are all being called to lead in our own ways . . . students who are coming up in the world, recent retirees, mothers and fathers, those in leadership who are challenged . . . we should all be able to see ourselves in the examples presented. No excuses!

"I thank him wholeheartedly for this beautiful contribution."

—Kelly Mellos, fine artist/author/speaker

"In a time of unprecedented division and acrimony, the message of reconciliation and forgiveness is now more important than ever. Born out of painful experience and a life of practice, Azim Khamisa is both a messenger and role model of the practice of forgiveness and reconciliation. Azim has touched the lives of people across the globe and across the spectrum, from school kids, to business and governmental leaders. This is a must read for those looking for inspiration and wishing to help mend a seemingly confused world."

—Dustin Seale, Heidrick Consulting, Managing Partner EMEA

"In his latest book, *Leadership For the Greater Good*, Azim Khamisa offers a daring new visionary model of enlightened leadership to help us course correct toward a world that can work for everyone. This model adds the potent competencies of spirit, soul, and emotional intelligence to prevailing models that focus primarily on intellectual intelligence and career-oriented job-training skills.

"Khamisa shares his inspiring personal journey, including the stories of men and women who have shaped his character. All are exemplars of Satyagrahi leadership. This is highly recommended reading for those who seek to grow in wisdom and Truth. It is a must read for all who aspire to lead."

—Diane Temple

"As a soulful leader and humanitarian, Azim Khamisa excels at walking his talk. In *Leadership for the Greater Good*, he shares enduring wisdom and profiles the role models that gave him the fortitude to turn pain into love, make outstanding contributions to society, and become the leader the world needs him to be. This is what the world needs from all of us. Read and learn."

—Claudia Welss, Chairman, Institute of Noetic Sciences

"Exceptional people change the world through their leadership that is informed by their own vulnerability. When we take a close look at the people who touch and shape our hearts, we will discover most of them were at some point deeply wounded in their hearts. They are inspiring leaders because they allowed their wounds to become the source of their calling. Azim is one of the most inspiring leaders I have met. Azim is relentless in using his deepest wound as a source for the good. In this new book he portrays other leaders that have walked a similar although a different and inspiring path. This book is a compelling and must read for every leader who dares to learn how they can use their own life journey as a force for positive transformation. It is possible: a workplace, a school, a world where compassion is the foundation of every growth. Isn't that worth the investment?"

—Jakob van Wielink, executive coach, author of *Loss, Grief, and Attachment in Life Transitions* (Routledge), faculty mentor at the Portland Institute for Loss and Transition and partner at the School for Transition, the Netherlands

# LEADERSHIP FOR
# THE GREATER GOOD

*A Guide for Truth to Power Champions*

## AZIM KHAMISA

Printed in the United States of America

First Printing, 2020

ISBN-13: 978-1-949001-06-8 print edition
ISBN-13: 978-1-949001-07-5 ebook edition

Waterside Productions
2055 Oxford Ave
Cardiff, CA 92007
www.waterside.com

# DEDICATION

● ● ● ● ● ● ● ●

*To my mama, Remy Khamisa, a true satyagrahi leader who inspired this book by her passing on April 28, 2017. Mama, you are loved and remembered by the many people you touched in the eighty-seven years of your life that you dedicated to serving your community. I am so very proud to be your son! You were and are the rock of my life! Love you dearly!*

Dear Bambos :

thanks for your leadership!

*[signature]*

April 2025

# CONTENTS

Introduction                                                                xiii

Chapter 1   Azim Khamisa, From Murder to Forgiveness              1

Chapter 2   Ignatius of Loyola, From Sinner to Saint             18

Chapter 3   His Highness Prince Karim Aga Khan IV,
            Exemplary Business, Philanthropic, and Spiritual Leader   28

Chapter 4   Mata Amritanandamayi (Amma), The Hugging Saint      38

Chapter 5   Elie Wiesel, Breaking the Silence                   52

Chapter 6   Mubarak Awad, Promoting Nonviolence
            and Peace in Palestine                               66

Chapter 7   Daisaku Ikeda, A Champion of Practical Application
            of Buddhist Humanism                                 80

Chapter 8   Wilma Mankiller, Rebuilding a Broken Nation         88

Chapter 9   Kazuo Inamori, A Devout Spiritual Entrepreneur
            and Generous Philanthropist                          98

Chapter 10  Remy Khamisa, In Memory of Mama                     105


Conclusion                                                      127
Acknowledgments                                                 153

# INTRODUCTION

This is a different kind of leadership book than you may be used to reading. Although many have written books on leadership, and the leadership "gurudom" has many pundits, people still ask—myself included—Why do we seem to be experiencing a decline in effective leaders in our government agencies, for-profit and nonprofit corporations, institutes of higher learning, and religious organizations? In my view, we have had a serious leadership deficit for the last several decades. As a result, we are currently in a downward spiral of fake news, spin, lies, innuendo, divisiveness, violence, and threats of new wars.

Do you wonder, like me, "What happened to 'the Truth'?"

In this book I dive into this question through the stories of world-renowned leaders, many of whom come from outside the business world or the social sector. This is intentional: leaders reside in all sectors of society, from unsung, hard-working, stay-at-home moms and dads to social enterprise leaders to heads of family-run businesses to teachers, spiritual leaders, artists, and former felons. **No matter what type of leadership you practice, or if you are just beginning your leadership journey, every leader can grow intellectually, socially, and spiritually. That's what this book is about. It is part memoir, part historical**

**narrative, and part guidebook, with the aim of helping you investigate how you can lead better through inspirational stories of leaders who have competency in their technical fields, in their social contexts, and in their spiritual development.**

I would argue that the power of truth remains crucial, yet it has seemingly become more and more concealed. When someone lies, the listener can intuitively recognize it, shut down, and stop listening. In contrast, when we hear the truth, it impacts us at a deep level and resonates with our spirit! Our ears perk up, and our listening becomes focused and more attentive.

Leaders throughout history have recognized the importance of truth. In the Bible verse John 8:32, Lord Jesus Christ said, "Then you will know truth, and the truth will set you free" (New International Version). Similarly, Indian leader Mahatma Gandhi brought the might of the British Empire to its knees by pursuing a revolutionary truth through his nonviolent rebellion, a practice he called *satyagraha*.

*Satyagraha* means "insistence on truth," "loyalty to the truth," or "holding on to truth or truth force," which was embodied most clearly during the last century's nonviolent resistance and civil rights movements. Gandhi's satyagraha practice famously influenced many exemplary leaders in history, such as Martin Luther King Jr. in the United States, but today we see very few satyagrahis in politics, religion, the corporate world, nonprofits, and universities. The premise of this book challenges our current models of leadership development. Today, most leadership models singularly emphasize improving one's chosen field of endeavor, but there should be so much more to a leader than career. We have become so focused on being "the best" that we are constantly living in our heads, worried about providing for ourselves and our families, and reluctant to acknowledge the problems that do not directly involve us. The world desperately needs leaders who can address our planet's most pressing dilemmas, including poverty, immigration, crime, violence, divisiveness, environmental issues, and the loss of democracy, as well as the need for freedom and inclusiveness. As concerned, caring citizens we must spawn a new breed of leaders to face them.

The strength of my model, unlike other models out there on leadership, is that the kind of leaders we need to spawn today need to have competencies in three separate disciplines and *not* only in their chosen career. We humans do not just live in our homes and work—we also live in and are an integral part of our respective communities.

My leadership model posits that today's leaders will need equal competencies in three different disciplines:

1) **Competency in our chosen fields**, whether in engineering, law, medicine, business, architecture, education, nonprofit work, justice, government, mothers and fathers, citizens, and other fields of endeavors that make our global society and economy work. We must strive to create a global society that works for all. That is the best security and a precursor to world peace. An academic resume alone, however, does not fulfill the job description for tomorrow's leaders.

2) **Equal competency in tackling societal issues** that make our respective communities a better place to live. This requires going beyond just filling individual bank accounts to fulfilling the wider needs of the community. From the Christian scriptures we are taught, "Love your neighbor as yourself," and in Hinduism, "Do not do to others what you would not have them do to you," as well as countless examples from other religions. Our relationships and concerns must include our community and not just ourselves, families, and close friends. We do not just live in our homes or in gated subdivisions—we live in our entire communities. This includes both sides of the track! To make communities thrive, we

require capable leaders in all sectors—leaders who portray the capability and passion to take on societal challenges of their communities and develop effective, viable, and affordable solutions.

3) **An unwavering adherence to a well-developed moral, ethical, and spiritual competency** that embraces strong values such as truth, empathy, compassion, love, service, and community. Spiritual competence does not necessarily translate to adhering to a certain faith or religion. The spirit is the voice that speaks beyond our own, guiding us to make the best decision based on our personal morals and ethics. These quintessential values—like nature and gravity—will always prevail. While all faiths teach these universal spiritual values, few leaders adhere to them. Leaders strong in spiritual competency attempt to integrate the intellectual, moral, social, and spiritual aspects of their lives. While no one succeeds all the time, leaders persevere in integrating all aspects of themselves.

**Fortunately, we have a few genuine satyagrahi leaders in our world, but they, and we, need many more like them. We face a critical time in our history, and our time proves short.**

On a positive note, millennials in the United States and abroad have begun to invest more attention in societal issues and spiritual values rather than just the relentless pursuit of the almighty dollar and personal pleasure, as practiced in the yuppie era. This book embodies the hopes and prayers for a new generation, whatever its label, to tackle the problems they must own. It aims to draw lessons from selected past leaders in order to arm future leaders with the skills they will need to solve tomorrow's complex problems.

Innumerable books and essays have been written on various styles of leadership. One of my favorite leadership models is the servant-leader model as described in *The Understanding and Practice of Servant Leadership*, by Larry C. Spears of the Greenleaf Center for Servant Leadership. Spears writes, "Servant-leadership deals with the reality of power in everyday life—its legitimacy, the ethical restraints upon it, and the beneficial results that can be attained through the appropriate use of power."

This model refers to a set of ten characteristics of the servant-leader that I view as being of critical importance. The following characteristics are central to the development of servant-leaders: Listening, Empathy, Healing, Awareness, Persuasion, Conceptualization, Foresight, Stewardship, Commitment, and Building Community.

While these ten characteristics of servant-leadership do not cover all the do's and don'ts needed by tomorrow's leaders, they serve to communicate the power and promise that this concept offers to those open to its invitation and challenge.

There are other models, for example, the seminal work done by Angela Lee Duckworth, where she researched a plethora of students and professionals to see what attributes would help them succeed. She is a renowned psychologist who has studied students, teachers, military personnel, corporate leaders, and others to determine what qualities predict successful leaders. Interestingly, in none of the cases was it IQ—even though most all institutions use this measure as a predictor of success. It was "grit," which she describes as the power of passion and perseverance. She explains that those who succeed possess a growth mind-set and look to the long term. Each failure is a stepping stool to the next step, and that success is not a sprint but a marathon. With passion, perseverance, and a growth mind-set, leaders do often achieve the worthy goals they set for themselves.

Another one of my favorites is a well-known book on leadership, *Good to Great*, by James C. Collins. In this book he cites several corporations that have consistently beaten the norms of their industries by many folds. Here are some of the strategies they use:

- Level 5 Leadership: Choose leaders who are humble but driven to do what's best for the company.
- First Who, Then What: Get the right people on the bus, then figure out where to go. Find the right people and try them out in different seats on the bus (different positions in the company).
- Confront the Brutal Facts: Face the reality of the situation, yet at the same time, never give up hope. This is also known as the Stockdale paradox.
- Hedgehog Concept: Your path to greatness lies at the intersection of three overlapping circles—What lights your fire ("passion")? What could you be the best at in the world ("best at")? What makes you money ("driving resource")?
- Culture of Discipline: Learn to "rinse the cottage cheese," or trim the fat, to determine what's truly essential.
- Technology Accelerators: Use technology to accelerate growth, within the three circles of the hedgehog concept.
- The Flywheel: The additive effect of many small initiatives; they act on each other like compound interest.

The qualities above that can be enacted by anyone wanting to grow his or her leadership practice are showing Level 5 Leadership, the Flywheel, and a Culture of Discipline. Imagine leaders enacting these principles in social contexts that require completely innovative solutions to intractable, wicked social problems! Another model of leadership that seems important at this time is *Primal Leadership*, by Daniel Goleman, Richard Boyatzis, and Annie McKee, which proposes that leaders must use other kinds of intelligence than IQ to be effective and successful. This is the book that established "emotional intelligence" in the business lexicon—and made it a necessary skill for leaders. Managers and professionals across the globe have embraced *Primal Leadership*, affirming the importance of emotionally intelligent leadership. Its influence has also reached well beyond the business world: the book and its ideas are now used routinely in universities, business and medical schools, professional training programs, and by a growing legion of professional coaches. Don't you agree that leadership that is self-aware, empathic, motivating, and collaborative is critical to produce outcomes that are of the highest good for all concerned, as opposed to a leadership style that is socially, culturally, economically, and technologically volatile and complex?

I strongly urge you to study these books, as they are packed with wisdom and brilliant ideas on how to supercharge your leadership abilities. They have helped me develop my leadership acumen. There are too many more to mention, but a quick perusal of the *New York Times* Best Sellers list will give you plenty to read on the topic of leadership.

**This begs the question: With so many leadership books available, why is another one needed? How is my book different?**

Going back to the three competencies, many of the leadership books, including the above, demonstrate the importance of intellectual and technical skills, with tips to honing these skills. **I am introducing additional leadership competencies, or qualities, that are needed to change our world and address the plethora of societal challenges we find ourselves caught in.**

**The first is the importance of taking these honed leadership skills and making an equal commitment to address the societal challenges that exist in all communities with the same vigor and integrity as we do in our own chosen careers and endeavors.** While government and nonprofit **sectors** of our society do address societal challenges that many of us are concerned about, effective leaders in business and technical professions can be substantially more effective in solving these challenges by creating innovative, effective, viable, and affordable solutions, as this is what they do in their own professions and workplaces. In previous books and in my own work, I have tried to address the malaise of youth violence as a result of losing my only son to a senseless gang initiation at the hands of a fourteen-year-old gang member. The question I had to ask myself—and the question that catalyzed an alternative and more comprehensive view of leadership—was, "How did we create a society where children kill children?" I began to believe that if violence was a learned behavior, then nonviolence could also be learned. Taking on this challenge, I founded the Tariq Khamisa Foundation (more in Chapter 1), which is in its twenty-fifth year. The TKF has created an effective, viable, and affordable solution to one of the biggest malaises in our society—youth violence. **While I had no training in social services, I did possess the leadership skills to take on this challenge and create a solution.** Similarly, our future leaders need to bring their expertise and passion to address societal issues that seem unsolvable.

**The second piece in my model is to inspire future leaders to strongly espouse and model strong moral, ethical, and spiritual values.** In my own case, I have experienced that the spiritual inner guidance I receive through my daily two-hour meditation practice has singularly trumped IQ and EQ—maybe call it SQ for Spirituality Quotient. (My daily meditation is fully described at azimkhamisa.com, along with a guided meditation called "Manifesting Your Goals.") I believe we all have the answers to our most challenging questions, and once we build our lives on the foundation of strong moral, ethical, and spiritual values, these answers give us clarity and guidance. The important and critical takeaway here is that these quintessential values of truth, empathy, compassion, love, service, and community are in concert with what many religions hold as their most cherished principles. This understanding is similar to the Dalai

Lama's proposal related to a set of secular ethics that could enhance world peace. Universal values can provide the resolve and the strength of character and will to accomplish great things in your life. While we all have access to these hidden and some might call "mystical" strengths, many of us have been taught to rely on logic/reason and science. Many of us in the West do not rely on these intangible values and tend to find answers through our intellect or through our emotions. **Although I attended premier English schools and was very invested in my education, my knowledge of mathematics and finance was useless when I had to deal with my deepest crisis—losing my only son in a tragic death. What saved me was my strong spiritual foundation and trust in my spirit to guide me to the work that I have done in the aftermath of this tragedy.**

Adherence to these essential moral, ethical, and spiritual values will also steer you away from malice so that you will not destroy yourself, your family, and your community. Think about the most vilified person in the twentieth century: Hitler. He accomplished massive social change with huge perseverance, but to the world's detriment and horror. What obviously was missing in him is the important value of compassion. His Holiness the Dalai Lama has suggested that the world should have only one religion: let us call it kindness. He has consistently asserted that human nature is at its best when it is grounded in compassion. On a lighter note, when I met the Dalai Lama for the first time, he shared that "a tiger's nature is to be aggressive; that is why a tiger has fangs and claws. We humans, our true nature is to be compassionate. That is why we have pretty teeth and nails!"

**Once you get the faculty of inner guidance from the higher power, it lives deeply in you beyond intellect and emotion. You tap into this reservoir of love and compassion. Your life will be more meaningful, more fulfilling, happier, and healthier.**

The journey I have been on has been immeasurably strengthened and enriched through my interaction with many wonderful individuals and organizations. I am honored and blessed to be serving as the board vice chair of the Institute of Noetic Sciences (IONS) (noetic.org), which was founded forty-six years ago by Edgar Mitchell, an astronaut who, as part of the Apollo 14 mission, set records for the longest distance traveled and the longest time spent walking on the moon. On his way back to Earth, Edgar had a window seat. As described by Elizabeth Howell: "He intuitively sensed that his presence, that of his fellow astronauts, and that of the planet in the window were all part of a deliberate, universal process and that the glittering cosmos itself was in some way conscious. The experience was so overwhelming, Edgar knew his life would never be the same."

This led him to start IONS, and for the last forty-six years IONS has been studying consciousness and its impact on our lives. At IONS we research outer limits and inner spaces to reveal a deeper understanding of the interconnected nature of reality and in so doing extend our capacities as humans. This is huge, as most astronauts are scientists, and many will not believe in a deity or higher power without proof that God exists. But innately we know we are more than head and heart—we also are souls. Edgar connected with this reality, and we now are studying the frontiers of consciousness: meditation, distance healing, shamanic practices, precognition, and other noetic experiences we have all had but don't routinely rely on in our daily living and work. I believe strongly that connecting with this innate wisdom will lead future leaders to create a world that works for everyone.

Finally, another attribute that has immensely helped me is to have amazing role models. In this book I discuss some of them in detail and discuss others who helped me during some very challenging times. While not everyone has suffered a major calamity like I did, at some level almost all people's hearts have been broken. I always strongly recommend that in your evolution you surround yourself with exemplary role models and coaches and seek inner guidance. My own philosophy is CANEI, which is the acronym for "constant and never-ending improvement." I am better today than I was yesterday and will be better the day after than I am tomorrow: this is a concept that W. Edwards Deming helped instill, especially in post–World War II Japan, when it rose from the ashes of war to become the behemoth it is today. In other words, adopt a growth mind-set. So when you read the following chapters, keep these three competencies in your backdrop, as you will see strong manifestations of these attributes in all of these brilliant leaders.

At the end of each chapter, I have listed questions that I have pondered in reaction to the lives of the leaders I profiled in this book. You will have your own questions you can use to reflect on, based on what you have learned from leaders in your life. I hope that these questions spur you to reflect on how others in your life have positively contributed to your knowledge about the world and yourself, and spur you on further to develop into the satyagrahi leader you want to be.

And that is why a new model of leadership is needed—one that exists beyond monthly metrics, sales quotas, and end-of-year reports. Leadership in its deepest sense is embodied in personal qualities that exist outside of our professional lives and live moment by moment in every decision we make. These decisions are vastly influenced by role models and self-reflection. This book is a guidebook for thinking about leadership and reflecting on your own capacity to be a leader in your areas of expertise for the good of your local community and the wider world. As you read this book, think about which leaders in your life come to mind for you. At the end of the book, you will have a chance to reflect further on who these leaders are, how they have made you reflect on your life, and how your own strengths relate to your role models and these questions.

# 1
## AZIM KHAMISA
## FROM MURDER TO FORGIVENESS

*"We humans encounter many defining moments in our lives. Some are joyous, and some are heartbreakingly devastating. At these moments, if we are able to make the right choice, we literally manifest a miracle and transformation in our lives and others."*

—*Azim Khamisa*

My biggest revelation is that, throughout our lives, we humans get challenges that cannot be solved with intellect alone. Albert Einstein reminds us, "We should take care not to make the intellect our God; it has, of course, powerful muscles, but no personality. It cannot lead, it can only serve." This insight is from the preeminent intellect of the previous century, but it can still be effortlessly applied to our situations here in the present. I have also discovered that there will be tragedies one's heart simply cannot mend—sometimes emotions like anger, fear, guilt, or regret can critically restrict the healing process. But I have come to the conclusion that there are *no* problems your spirit cannot solve or heal. But first you must have a strong spiritual foundation. It took me a while before I was able to live beyond my head and my heart and trust in my spirit, but now that I know its might, I completely trust in my soul and will lead from there.

## In Africa

I was born in 1949 in a small town called Kisumu in Western Kenya, the largest port on Lake Victoria that cradles Kenya, Uganda, and Tanzania, collectively referred to as East Africa. From 1920 to 1963 Kenya was a British colony; the key official government positions were manned by British citizens. As a result, many policies put into place during this time disregarded the needs and desires of the indigenous population. Most Kenyans were illiterate, as the country lacked an organized education system. In order to fill the middle management government positions, the ruling British gave incentives to literate people in their other controlled colonies, such as India, to transfer to Kenya and work. My paternal grandfather, an entrepreneur and risk-taker, took advantage of this opportunity and moved to Kenya from India when he was thirteen years old. A few generations prior, my other forefathers had also migrated to India, this time to escape the religious persecution taking place in Persia. As a result, I was raised to appreciate both Indian and Persian culture from different sides of my family.

I was raised in the Ismaili faith, a denomination in the Sufi tradition of Islam. The then Aga Khan—the leader and imam of the fifteen million Ismailis—was one of the ousted leaders in Persia who sought India for refuge (see Chapter 4). Growing up, I wanted to be like the Aga Khan—successful, generous, a loved leader through and through. He was, and remains, my most influential role model. So, like him, it was important to me to develop a strong spiritual foundation at a young age. In my Ismaili tradition, we refer to our place of prayer as Jamat Khana, which also doubles up as a gathering place for social and other community events outside of prayers. Jamat Khana was very much part of my daily life—every evening my family and I attended for evening prayers. As a young man I also participated in organizing events and holiday celebrations, was chairman of the youth council, and was in charge of the social work within the organization.

But my most memorable moment within the organization—within my life, really—was meeting the Aga Khan. I had organized a five-star dinner for the visit, the most elaborate event our religious community had ever seen. Every detail was accounted for—the beautiful plating of the five courses to be served, the roles to be played by each of the forty waiters, even the gold trim of the glassware to be used by the Aga Khan himself. But once the Aga Khan arrived, all the stress I experienced milling over fine details seemed pointless; his presence itself made everything feel so grand. I spoke with him only briefly, but his sincerity behind a simple "Hello" and "Thank you" was almost surprising; his powerful position did not distract him from his humanity. When I left my home for America, I never forgot this encounter—over the years I have served in many roles in the Ismaili community with hopes of impacting the world through selflessness and good deeds as he did.

I attended grade school in Kenya—a beautiful country to grow up in, with frequent visits of deer and gazelles in my backyard. It was also the home of elephants (my favorite animal), lions, giraffes, rhinos, cheetahs, zebras, and countless other species of wild animals, birds, and fauna. If you have not yet experienced an African safari, I suggest you add it to your bucket list—I have been fortunate to experience many safaris over the years, each one as revolutionary as the last. In 1963 Kenya won its independence from Britain, and my family and I were able to become naturalized Kenyan citizens.

Growing up, I was blessed to have been exposed to so many cultures. I have always maintained that my worldview was developed from the cultures I experienced living in Kenya as a little boy. Africa has a very rich soul, and as we are discovering, there is much wisdom in aboriginal cultures. I have witnessed firsthand their fierce loyalty, strong sense of community, and undeniable connection to nature.

We grew up with servants; my servant, Victor, was the son of my parents' servant, Pedro. We were the same age, so we grew up together and were very good friends. When we were young, we'd play soccer together, our connection to the earth and soil evident underneath our muddy bare feet. We'd share secrets and stories, confide in each other, and laugh and laugh together. When my family decided to leave Kenya and head west for America, Victor was very distraught, as I was not only his friend but his livelihood. My family supported him and his family of three wives and six children and took care of all their needs, including medical care. He wanted to move to the United States with me, but I told him the transition might be too difficult for him and his family—they could not read, write, or speak English, and the cultural shock alone would likely be a huge barrier for them. But he was adamant that he should continue to serve my family in America, even offering to leave his own behind in Kenya and visit them just once a year. I assured him the new buyers of our family business would provide him a job with equal benefits, but Victor could not trust them with his and his family's well-being; they were members of two different tribes with an unstable relationship.

I knew Victor was extremely loyal to me, and I have no doubt he would have put his body between a bullet and me if it ever were the case. So, not wanting to leave my friend with an unpredictable future, I ended up buying him a modest farm, large enough to grow corn and a few other crops, plant fruit trees such as mango and papaya (my favorite), and raise cattle. With this farm, the family could be self-sustainable. I remember I had only $30,000 to my name when I moved to the United States, and I used a third of it to purchase him the farm, even though I got a lot of flak for it from my family and friends! But I never once regretted my decision—I could rest easy knowing he and his family were well taken care of.

Victor became an accomplished farmer growing crops and raising cattle, as well as a well-respected member in his community. A generous soul, he always looks for a way to help anyone when he can. I believe he gives more of his crops away than he sells! Whenever I visit Kenya, they hold a big feast in my honor, forever thanking me for my generosity. But his true gift to me was knowing that he and his family were happy, and that I had contributed to that happiness. I have learned in my journey that the deep connections I enjoy with my soul were a gift from Africa and my relationship with Victor.

In Kenya my grandfather did well and ran several passenger buses for transporting locals to the various villages and towns around Kisumu. After a heated argument between him and my father, my father left home, went to work for an automobile company, and later started his own automobile dealership with two other partners. The dealership was a franchise for Peugeot, a French car manufacturer popular in East Africa. The business flourished, and while my genesis was to be born poor, by the time I was in my adolescent years my family was doing well and was able to afford my English education.

After graduating from grade school in 1964 at the early age of fifteen, I spent the next six years in England as a college student studying mathematics and finance. These formative years of my life were an introduction and immersion into British and European culture, where I learned to speak English. In college I aced my accounting courses, finishing at the top and passing a test that only 18 percent of eighteen thousand students passed. If things had gone smoothly and according to plan, perhaps I would not have become an African entrepreneur.

But in 1971 I had to interrupt my studies in England and return to Kenya to take over my father's business as he battled a serious heart condition. In Muslim families, the eldest son is expected to continue supporting his family when his father cannot, so I returned, acknowledging that it was my duty. I was twenty-one years old and expected to manage a business with one hundred employees—I had to learn to be an entrepreneur at a young age.

At that time Japanese cars were beginning to enter the market, and although I was anxious from the growing competition, I recalled one of the most important lessons I had learned from my favorite professor, Dr. Harvey: "You're looking over your shoulder to see who's catching up with you. You should be catching up to the person in front of you." With his advice in mind, I expanded the scope of the business to include automobile-related financial services: leasing, lending, and insurance. Miraculously, I doubled our profits in the next eighteen months, and we were on a profitable growth cycle until Idi Amin, a violent dictator in neighboring Uganda, took power and destabilized the entire region.

Idi Amin expelled all non-indigenous people living in Uganda, among whom were my mother's family and my in-laws. I had married early in 1971 at the age of twenty-two to Almas and welcomed my daughter,

Tasreen, at age twenty-three. The rise of Idi Amin brought our life, as well as the lives of thousands of immigrants, to a crashing halt. Many nonindigenous people in the East African countries began emigrating to the West in search of safety and peace.

## To America

Since I was educated in Europe and could speak and write English, my family decided that it was befitting we also leave Africa to begin a new life in the West; however, we had to sell the family business first, a complicated sale, as most qualified buyers were also leaving the country. After two challenging years, I was finally able to complete a complex sale to a local African group for a healthy cash price, to the chagrin of my father and his two partners. I was unaware at the time that this sale would be my first experience as an investment banker, the profession I would soon be pursuing in the Western world.

At age twenty-five, my family and I moved first to Canada and then to the United States, where I believed I'd have plentiful opportunities to pursue my new career. During our short stay in Canada, my second child and son, Tariq, was born. Not long after, my entire family relocated to Seattle, Washington.

The physical relocation took just a few months, but adapting to a new lifestyle and culture proved much more strenuous. Believing I had finally made it to the land where all my desires could be fulfilled, I became engulfed with material conquests. I stopped caring about my health, my spiritual well-being, and the relationships I had with my loved ones. My wife and I decided to divorce after ten years of marriage, as my priorities had deteriorated. It wouldn't be until I lost almost everything that I had earned in risky investments that I would realize it was time to refocus. I moved to Atlanta in search of a change of pace and started my own investment banking consulting firm, but in 1988 I permanently relocated to the quaint beach city of La Jolla, California.

I maintained an amicable relationship with Almas, Tasreen, and Tariq as they continued their lives 1,250 miles away in Seattle. We often spoke on the phone, spent holidays and summers together, and I'd travel to see them every three months, but I missed so many soccer games, award ceremonies, first heartbreaks, and other life-changing events. I found it difficult to be the father my kids felt they could turn to—the physical distance proved to be a strong barrier. Luckily, Tariq gave me the chance to prove myself when he decided to attend college at San Diego State University, just a few miles from my home. We would often get breakfast before work and classes, catching up on my latest business ventures and his relationship with his girlfriend, Jennifer. When he decided to pursue a degree in art rather than follow in my footsteps as a businessman, he thought I'd be devastated and angry. But in his few short years at college, I watched my son become a man who I believed would do great things, whether he pursued them in a suit or behind the lens of a Canon DSLR. As father, friend, and mentor, I supported my son as he paved a new path for himself.

Unfortunately, that path was much too short.

## Tragedy and Peace

In 1995 my life took a devastating blow—Tariq, who worked weekends as a pizza delivery boy, was lured to a bogus address by a youth gang and was shot and killed by fourteen-year-old Tony Hicks, who sought to prove himself in a gang initiation ritual. I didn't believe the homicide detective when she told me the news; I thought, "You must be mistaken, ma'am; it couldn't have been Tariq. My son was a good person—a bit hardheaded at times, but he'd never get himself into a dangerous situation like this."

Of course, it didn't matter how much I wanted the detectives to be wrong. Tariq was gone—he was just twenty years old! Needless to say, life seemed to stop as I struggled to process the horrific news. I went through all the emotions a parent would suffer losing a child: hopelessness, despair, overwhelming and unbearable grief—I was suicidal at one point as I wrestled with the fact that I would never see my son again, would never tousle his hair again, would never hear him laugh, would never have the opportunity to witness the man he would have become. I did not know how to go forward with my life without Tariq. I had gone through many trials and tribulations thus far and had always managed to land on higher ground. But this time I had no tools at my disposal to handle the loss of my only son. I had to completely surrender myself to God before I was able to slowly start picking up the pieces.

In deep tragedy, however, there is a spark of clarity—every saint has suffered a dark night of the soul. Even at this moment of devastating loss, I realized that there were victims at both ends of the gun. As Henry David Thoreau once said, "The question is not what you look at, but what you see." I was able to take a step back and recognize that the enemy was not the fourteen-year-old who had killed my son, but rather the societal forces that coerce many young souls—especially those of color—to fall through the cracks into lives of gangs, crime, drugs, alcohol, and guns.

Yes, it is easy to see that Tariq was a victim of the fourteen-year-old gang member, Tony. A little harder is to see that Tony was a victim of society—of American society. We Americans are responsible for the society we have created, and as a first-generation naturalized American citizen, I felt I must accept my share of the responsibility for the bullet that took my son's life. Why? Because it was fired by an American child.

Nine months after Tariq's death, I decided the grieving stage was over—it was time to take action. In honor of my son, I founded the Tariq Khamisa Foundation. Our mission initially was threefold:

1. to save the lives of children, as we lose way too many on a daily basis, either to an untimely death, like Tariq, or to the criminal justice system, like Tony;

2.  to empower youth to make the right choices and understand the consequences of choosing a life of crime, violence, gangs, drugs, and weapons; and

3.  to teach the principles of nonviolence—empathy, compassion, forgiveness, and peacemaking.

I began with a simple premise—that violence is a learned behavior, and that if you accept it as an axiom, then nonviolence can also be a learned behavior. But this must be physically taught to children, as they will not understand the principles of nonviolence simply through osmosis. TKF now has a comprehensive safe school model that encompasses four separate programs under its umbrella that, with the grace of God, has shown exemplary results. The programs include: (1) a live Peacemaker assembly with Tony's grandfather and me followed by a debrief of how to transform negative emotions into positive ones; (2) a ten-week curriculum on restorative practices that teaches accountability, empathy, compassion, forgiveness, and community engagement; (3) creation of a peace club on campus, which is a leadership training for community engagement; and (4) a mentoring program for the challenging kids. We have substantially expanded TKF's platform from our initial vision and are diligently engaged in serving youth in all our communities nationwide. You can learn more about it on my website at tkf.org.

Soon after starting TKF, I invited Tony's grandfather and guardian, Ples Felix, to join me with the notion that we both had lost a son. Ples had been raising Tony since he was nine years old—Tony called him "Daddy," and Ples worked tirelessly to foster a loving relationship. When I met him, I told him I was reaching out to him in compassion and forgiveness rather than revenge and retribution. While I couldn't bring Tariq back from the dead, and Ples couldn't reverse Tony's life sentence, the one thing we could jointly do was make sure no other young person ended up in either situation. Ples was quick to take my hand, and with God's grace the foundation has been discouraging youth around the country from pursuing a life of violence and crime for twenty-four years.

Since TFK's founding, I have given over a thousand presentations to students worldwide on the principles of nonviolence and the importance of compassion, inspiring them to become global leaders who follow the tenets of this book. That is to say, I strive to influence these students to possess super-competency in their chosen field of endeavor, commit themselves to solving societal issues, and develop and adhere to strong spiritual, ethical, and moral values. These live presentations have reached over a million millennials; what gives me much hope is that these principles are not only teachable, but the youth seem hungry for a path paved with empathy and good deeds, a path some would have never been introduced to without TKF.

Besides our live presentations, TKF's message has been distributed to millions more through school broadcasts; several local, national, and international media interviews on television, radio, and print; and through my books and many other books that carry my story. I have also organized an extensive international speaking schedule with over seven hundred keynote addresses to adults who work with youth and/or run for-profit and nonprofit corporations, institutes of higher learning, spiritual venues of all faiths, and social justice professionals. Many of the students, youth, and adults inspired by my message have written to me; I have received over one hundred thousand letters expressing their gratitude and revelations sparked by TKF's message. It gives me tremendous hope to see that they will become satyagrahi leaders.

With this new and life-altering perspective, I was able to face Tony five years after he had killed my son. I did not see an evil person when we met—when I looked into his eyes, I saw the same pain I saw in my own. He was struggling with the consequences of his actions, and not just with the fact that he would spend his foreseeable future in prison. He apologized from the bottom of his heart for the pain he had caused my family, for the senseless killing of my son. He asked for my forgiveness, and I (again) forgave him. And we were free.

## Lessons from My Satyagraha Journey

As a leader for the greater good I have learned the importance of cultivating the strength and resiliency to be able to always thrive, especially in times that are extremely challenging. Looking back at my life and the trials that I have overcome, the attributes that helped me land on higher ground each time—even through the devastating loss of my only son—are as follows:

1) Developing and preserving resiliency and vitality: When one contemplates vitality, one typically thinks of a good diet, exercise, yoga, meditation, prayer, and a good work-life balance. But there is more to vitality than developing these healthy habits. During my talks and workshops over the last twenty-four years, I have learned that everyone has a story. Many are in resentment due to what has been done to them or mired in guilt for the harm they have caused. At some level we, as fallible human beings, have caused harm and often to people who are closest to us. Resentment and guilt are highly debilitating states of emotions that gnaw on our conscience at all times, precluding us from performing at our full potential. Not performing to the best of our capabilities does not give deserved credit to ourselves, our families, or more importantly, to our community. If we are to transform the world we live in, all of us have a responsibility to perform at our full potential. To have true vitality it is important to forgive those who have harmed you so as to rid yourself of resentment, and equally important to

forgive yourself and thus rid yourself of guilt. I have chronicled this process in my books and workshops. I truly believe—even though I was not trained and educated in social services—that I have succeeded in all I've wanted to do because I do not harbor any resentment or guilt. Thus I can focus on my goals with a clear head, heart, and spirit. Forgiveness of others and of yourself will send your vitality, resiliency, and performance to a quantum level.

2) Living a life that is purpose driven: We all have a spiritual purpose in life, but sometimes it is difficult to understand what that purpose is. But we are nudged regularly by the Universe to steer us onto our path. Sometimes it is gentle guidance from loved ones, mentors, and friends. Sometimes it is an abrupt, life-altering revelation. I found my purpose in the tragedy of my son's death, compelling me to develop an affordable and viable solution to curb youth violence and to teach how to achieve peace through forgiveness. Over the last twenty-four years this message has touched millions around the world, and each year it continues to be heard. While I received no proper training in running a nonprofit, nor on public speaking or teaching, I have found that when you are on your spiritual pursuit you have a perpetual tail wind—the road rises to meet you. In other words, the Universe will provide you with support and the resources you need to fulfill your purpose. While it is difficult to know what one's purpose is, the best way to start searching is through service to your community. As Nobel Prize–winner Rabindranath Tagore once said, "I slept and dreamt that life was joy. I awoke and saw that life was service. I acted and behold, service was joy."

3) Having a growth mind-set and relying on inner guidance through spiritual alignment: I find that one can learn from those around them, even a child, and the ability to always be committed to life's

lessons is how one develops resiliency, effectiveness, and performance. Life is a mystery, and that is a good thing—if it were *not* a mystery, there would be no growth. What I have learned in my life's journey is, while you may not get a complete answer to the meaning of life, as you evolve, your questions get loftier, and in those questions is where growth manifests. I often get my "aha's!", or clarity, in my meditation practice. As I said earlier, intellect by itself is a limited faculty. It will justify anything, so left on its own it is not going to be able to provide deep wisdom. A friend of mine said, "A mind is a dangerous place to go by yourself."

There is nothing wrong with an intelligent mind if it is coupled with your heart and spirit. So when I have an important decision to make, I use the following process: (a) I go to my intellect and ask, "Does my decision make sense?" The intellect is effective at assessing the pros and cons of any situation, but beyond that it is limited. (b) If my decision does make sense in my head, I go to my heart, where emotions reside. "Does this decision feel right, just, or fair?" We all have a sense of what is moral. But I don't stop there, as there is no rudder in emotions—we all get carried away within our hearts. Often, we have done things that we felt made a lot of sense and felt really good, and later we come to regret it. That is because we don't realize there is a third step: (c) I go to my spirit and ask the question, "Is it inspiring? Will others follow my lead?" I grant you that using this process where you incorporate your head, heart, and soul will provide superior decisions that hold the best benefits for you, your situation, and the Universe. Spirit never makes a mistake—it is important to build your faith and trust unwaveringly in your spirit, as exemplified by other leaders showcased in this book.

I've been influenced a great deal by the cultures I've come across throughout my life. India, Persia, Africa, England, and America all had unique yet critical lessons to teach. As I said earlier, my roots are Eastern—my father was a businessman and my mother was very spiritual (see Chapter 10). I grew up in the Ismaili Sufi tradition, which has a wealth of wisdom and guidance. One such wisdom is the need for equality between one's material and spiritual life. For example, when I read a business book, I couple it with a spiritual book—a practice that I keep even today. I learned to meditate from one of my mother's close friends at the age of twenty—I currently meditate three separate times a day for a total of two hours every day. When Tariq was alive, it was only one hour a day—after I lost him the hours increased, as I had so much more to contemplate.

Having learned the might of the spirit through my tragedy, today I invite spirit into everything I do, as I know it is wiser and more powerful than intellectual or emotional intelligence. It was my spiritual foundation that helped me heal from the tragedy of my son's murder. At this deepest crisis in my life my education in mathematics and finance was useless, even though I had been educated at some fine schools in England. What saved me was my spiritual foundation, which was well chronicled in my book, *The Secrets of the Bulletproof Spirit: How to Bounce Back from Life's Hardest Hits*, coauthored by Jillian Quinn and published by Random House. Today I teach meditation; if you are interested, I have made available a free download on my website (www.azimkhamisa.com) about the methodology of my three-times-a-day, two-hour meditation practice, as well as two separate guided meditations on forgiveness and manifesting your goals. Meditation is an important tool for satyagrahi leaders desiring to build a foundation of strong spiritual values.

On the opposite side of the same coin, having lived in the Western world now for over forty-five years and also being educated in England, I have profited from learning much about material values in the West. In England I learned the importance of discipline, respect, etiquette, and presentation. In America I learned that through perseverance and hard work one can create an affordable, secure, and comfortable livelihood. I learned about freedom (something our brothers and sisters in other parts of the world do not enjoy), democracy, meritocracy, and independence. I have also witnessed firsthand the admirable examples of the millions of people who have dedicated their time, effort, and donations to provide services for those less fortunate. There is a rich network of nonprofit organizations and charities that seek to aid individuals with virtually any issue—from homelessness and poverty in America to genocide in Africa. There is a wealth of opportunity for anyone looking to get involved in an honorable cause. These values encompassed in Western societies can offer a great deal to a satyagrahi leader—I am amazed by what we have created in America in a short 240 years.

But there is one similarity among every culture I've discovered along my global journey: the overarching need and desire for peace among people. Our world has seen so much violence, so many scandals and devastating tragedies. Perhaps that's why I embarked on the path I chose. Tariq's death initially turned me inward, toward hopelessness. But I needed to turn outward, toward hope and light, for myself and for everyone I could reach. Toward peace.

Because I chose peace, I was able to give meaning to Tariq's life and his death. When I teach what it means to be a "peace leader" to the children and leaders not only in my own community but around the world, I have shed light when I could easily have spread darkness and hate. My only hope is that those who have taken the time to listen to my story will choose to spread light as well.

In conclusion, my worldview consists of living a lifestyle that is permanently shaped by the soul of Africa, the spiritual wisdom of the East, and the material wisdom of the West. It is important for satyagrahi leaders to listen to the world around them, to appreciate every culture and community, and to contemplate what can be learned from them. When we thoroughly understand each other, we can work together toward a better, more peaceful world.

## Question to Ponder:

The question to ask here is, "Are you fulfilled with your life as it exists?" When Tariq was alive, I spent most of my workday on my investment banking business, often working sixty to seventy hours a week and sometimes longer when closing a transaction. I did serve on some nonprofit boards and donated to charity, but it was a small part of my life. In the aftermath of Tariq's tragedy, the work that I have done in serving humanity has become a major portion of my day's work. I routinely volunteer twenty-five hours a week to my philanthropic work and am still able to maintain a simple but comfortable lifestyle. The big difference is, I feel far more fulfilled knowing that I am helping many young and old and will leave behind a strong legacy that will continue to help humanity for many years after I transition to the next life. That reminds me, once again, of the quote commonly attributed to Rabindranath Tagore: "I slept and dreamt that life was joy. I awoke and saw that life was service. I acted and behold, service was joy." Feeling this sense of fulfillment and peace comes from service. We are here to leave a better world for our children and grandchildren—I believe this is our moral duty.

# 2

## IGNATIUS OF LOYOLA
## FROM SINNER TO SAINT

*"Go forth and set the world on fire."*

*—Ignatius of Loyola*

Saint Ignatius of Loyola was once an arrogant man driven to achieve honor and fame through war as a skilled swordsman. The dream, however, died on the battlefield with a cannonball to his legs, a great tragedy that led Ignatius to rekindle his Catholic faith. He and a group of like-minded friends presented themselves to Pope Paul III to serve at his pleasure; this group came to be known as the Jesuits. The Jesuits vowed to work toward the greater good of society, but they left their most prominent mark on the education system, establishing one of the largest and oldest educational organizations in the world.

Born Iñigo López de Loyola in 1491, the man now known as Ignatius of Loyola entered the world in Loiola, Spain (also spelled "Loyola"). He was the youngest of thirteen children, his family a member of the local aristocracy. His mother died when Iñigo was just seven years old, and he was then raised by Maria de Garin, the wife of a blacksmith. Despite losing his mother, Loyola was still a member of the aristocracy and was raised accordingly in the castle of Loyola.

As a young man, Loyola dreamed of becoming a great leader. He was inspired by stories of heroism and bravery in war, such as *The Song of Roland* and *El Cid*. He joined the army at seventeen, but his vain and pompous demeanor was difficult to look past. According to biographers George Traub, SJ, and Debra Mooney, PhD, of Jesuitresource.org, Loyola was "a fancy dresser, an expert dancer, a womanizer, sensitive to insult, and a rough and punkish swordsman who used his privileged status to escape prosecution for violent crimes committed with his priest brother at carnival time." Iñigo also gained the reputation of a duelist, challenging and killing men who dared defy him, his family, or his Catholic faith. It was at this time that Loyola began referring to himself as "Ignatius" in hope of seeking wider acclaim, since Ignatius could be better understood in France and Italy.

In 1509, at the age of eighteen, Loyola took up arms for Antonio Manrique de Lara, Duke of Nájera. He fought in several battles under the leadership of the duke and had a talent for emerging unscathed. His diplomacy and leadership qualities earned him the title "servant of the court," and soon Loyola was granted command of his own troops.

But the rise to fame that Loyola so longed for was cut tragically short when a French-Navarrese expedition force stormed the fortress of Pamplona on May 20, 1521. A cannonball struck him in the legs, wounding his right leg and fracturing his left in multiple places. The injury was the end of his military career, and Loyola returned home, where he underwent several painful operations to repair his legs.

While recovering from his surgeries, Loyola read and reread a biography of the life of Christ and novels on the lives of the saints, the only reading material found in the castle. He was moved by the saints' service to God as a holy chivalry and found his past life and dreams detestable in comparison. After much reflection, he resolved to imitate the holy austerities of the saints in order to do penance for his sins.

In 1522 Loyola left home to begin his pilgrimage to Montserrat in northeastern Spain. Once there, he spent three days confessing his every sin and abandoned all symbols of his past life and ambitions. He next traveled to Manresa, a town thirty miles from Barcelona, to pass the decisive months of his career. He spent these months as a beggar, ate and drank sparingly, scourged himself, and hardly ever groomed. Every day he would attend mass followed by seven hours in prayer, often in a cave outside the city. His time in Manresa was marked by several spiritual trials accompanied by joy and awakening, inspiring him to begin his book, *The Spiritual Exercises*, which would later become an important manual for spiritual retreats.

Once Loyola had completed his pilgrimage, he decided to pursue the highest degree of education he could acquire in terms of the circumstances. He put off his priesthood for more than twelve years, deciding instead to enter the classroom at thirty-three, an age when most men had long completed their training, studying among young school-boys in Barcelona before proceeding to philosophy at the University of Alcalá. He was convinced a man who had acquired the necessary skills could accomplish in a short time what one without any training would never accomplish.

During his studies in Alcalá, Loyola began to attract a small group of followers. The group was exercised in the same exterior mortifications, begging, fasting, going barefoot, etc. that Ignatius had put himself through in Manresa. Unfortunately, he soon fell under suspicion of heresy. Loyola was imprisoned and tried for preaching without a degree but ultimately was found innocent. A similar event happened when Loyola left Alcalá for the University of Salamanca, but this time his disciples were apprehended as well. He decided then it was best that he abstain from public religious endeavor until he had reached the priesthood.

Eventually, Loyola earned his master's degree, and by the time he fin-ished his schooling he had also gained a background in theology and the science of education. Now believing he was qualified for his priesthood, Loyola gathered his companions who were to become the cofounders of the *Compañia de Jesús,* or the Society of Jesus. In Montmartre the group bound themselves by vows of poverty, chastity, and obedience, oblivious to the huge religious order they were to become. Unlike his first group of disciples in Alcalá, the Society adapted their dress and habits to life in Paris—fasting and other harsh disciplines were reduced, studies and spiri-tual exercises were increased, and alms were funded. Ignatius and most of his companions were ordained into the priesthood on June 24, 1537.

In 1539 Ignatius and the Society of Jesus decided to form a perma-nent union, and in 1540 Pope Paul III approved the plan of the new order, choosing Loyola for the office of Superior General.

The Society of Jesus developed rapidly under Loyola's lead. He began sending his companions as missionaries around Europe to "seek the greater glory of God" and the good of all humanity, creating schools, colleges, and seminaries in their wake. Soon a Jesuit college was established in Messina, Spain, which proved an immense success; its rules and methods served as a model for the Jesuits' future education system.

At the time of Loyola's death in 1556 there were one thousand Jesuits, most of them involved in the thirty-five schools that had been founded. Twenty-five years later that number rose to 144, and today that number has nearly quadrupled, with 374 secondary schools and 190 colleges worldwide. The Jesuit educational system is perhaps the strongest and most grounded education system in the world, having recently celebrated its five-hundred-year anniversary.

## Competency in His Field of Endeavor

Whether Loyola was pursuing fame and recognition as a hero of war or penance as a saint, his determination and willingness to go above what was expected of him earned him a place in the history books. The same competitive nature that fueled his quick temper as a young man was channeled into developing one of the most productive religious orders in the world.

His journey to priesthood was unconventional—as we learned in the last section, Loyola was forced to change his career path after his harrowing encounter on the battlefield, leaving him with a lifelong limp. But Loyola did not sulk for long! His misfortune was paired with a revelation, a second chance to start anew. He abandoned his entitled aristocratic life to pursue a closer relationship to God, inspiring others along the way.

At an age where most men had already found their place in society, Loyola began to lay the bricks of his legacy. He realized the value of a thorough education, so he swallowed his pride and went to study among children in grammar school at the age of thirty-three. But he was not satisfied with the bare necessities. Loyola went on to study theology and Latin at university—fields required for a priest—but throughout the ten years he dedicated to educating himself, Loyola traveled all over the world, taking classes in all sorts of academic areas, from liberal arts to philosophy, logic, physics, and education. He spent the most time at the University of Paris, a school known for its incredibly difficult curriculum, and graduated with a master of arts after seven years, earning him the title "Master Ignatius," as many would refer to him later in life. He would have pursued a doctorate, but his application was passed over because of his age and fears that his ailments could impact his studies. Regardless, he dedicated twelve years to furthering his education, believing a rich educational background would help him better serve God as well as the diverse worldly population he sought to inspire.

Loyola's commitment demonstrated at the University of Paris attracted a following of Europe's most talented scholars, who chose to rally behind a most unlikely character. Loyola was utterly lacking in conventional leadership credentials; he was thirty-eight—well into the twilight of an average sixteenth-century lifetime; he had failed his first career, had two arrests and multiple run-ins with the Spanish Inquisition, and no money. But the self-awareness and enlightenment he gained during his time in Manresa, as well as his natural leadership skills, overshadowed his flaws.

Once the Society of Jesus was formed, it took the group a while to find success. Loyola and his followers were dedicated to "helping souls," but no one really knew what that entailed. Their determination and creativity were admirable, but with no plan in place, the new organization was left volunteering at hospitals and preaching on street corners. But the quality of their modest efforts began to attract the attention of the Pope and other church officials, and soon the group was selected for scattered missions to preach or lecture. As members were sent across the globe, the Society of Jesus decided to become a new religious order with an elected superior general in order to keep the association from disintegrating. They were convinced that they must preserve the spirit that unified them, even as diverse missions separated them physically. Loyola was the obvious choice for general.

Loyola's time at university and his background in education inspired his leadership style once he was granted the title of superior general of the Society of Jesus. Some would describe his rule as almost military-like, a remnant of his past life as a soldier of war. But despite being strict, Loyola was organized, tactful, and dedicated to bettering his organization and those they encountered along their mission trips around the world. Much of their efforts were focused on furthering education, but members were prepared to engage in any occupation that would "help souls."

Perhaps what made Loyola most competent in his endeavors was his desire to instill the leadership qualities and self-awareness he possessed among his followers. The Society of Jesus was never designed to be a hierarchy—it appeared to become one once the Pope appointed Loyola as superior general—but each member was expected to lead their own mission and tasks of daily life. The Jesuits knew themselves; they emerged from their corporate prehistory with ideas about how they wanted to work as a team—driven by heroism, open to new opportunities, and tightly bound by mutual support. Loyola could not be in charge of every mission, nor could he control what was happening within branches of his organization in different countries. Education and self-examination were at the heart of the movement, and only after years of training was a Jesuit considered prepared to carry out his mission. Jesuits were expected to act in the same heroic way Loyola had when resolving to become a saint, always choosing a path toward the betterment of themselves and society. These lessons in leadership are taught in Jesuit schools and universities, and today many successful world leaders have graduated from the Jesuit educational system, demonstrating the same leadership qualities five hundred years after Loyola.

## Competency in Tackling Societal Issues

"Helping souls": the Jesuit mission Loyola originally stated is broad, encompassing all issues including poverty, hunger, homelessness, disaster relief, education, and everything in between. Loyola, unlike other priests during his time, was free-thinking and did not discriminate against people of different religions or backgrounds. His focus was mostly secular when aiding people through his missions and in his classrooms—the Jesuits tolerated students of other religions, taught other theology in their institutions, and believed in free education for all. Social and missionary work is a core value in Jesuit schools and universities, and each student is expected—if not required—to give back to society in their own way.

Loyola's legacy is, of course, the expansive and well-respected education system he began to establish during his lifetime. Today only about one percent of the world is able to receive a college education, and even fewer were able to receive one during Loyola's time.    Therefore, the Jesuits believe that the rest of the world is looking to those with an education to be able to make a difference in their lives. The Jesuits believed that by providing a more accessible educational system, it would inspire students to want more and to seek to live with enthusiasm. By teaching the liberal arts, sciences, and mathematics, a Jesuit education is designed to help students discover their passion as well as educate them on a variety of topics, preparing them for the diverse experiences they will encounter in the world. By providing the same groundwork in each school and university established around the world, the Jesuits hope to unify their students in the principles of dedication, philanthropy, and leadership.

The Jesuit school has been around for five hundred years, compared to sixteen of the one hundred American companies formed in the year 1900 that managed to survive long enough to celebrate their one hundredth anniversary. It has coped with a complex, changing environment, becoming the world's largest religious order with twenty-one thousand professionals running two thousand institutions in more than one hundred countries.

## Competency in Spirit

Perhaps the most notable lesson one can discern from Loyola's iconic life journey is the ability to reinvent oneself. Despite the most devastating of tribulations that seemingly crushed his dreams of notoriety, Loyola was able to find inspiration elsewhere. Far past his prime and left wounded with a lifelong injury, many men in Loyola's situation would have lost sight of redemption.

Without the setbacks, crises, and challenges that punctuated his life, Loyola might never have grappled with who he was, what he wanted, what personal resources he had, and why he had failed along the way. He turned his despair into personal reflection—he did not dwell on the negatives but worked to change them into positives. In doing so he strengthened that invaluable connection with his soul and gained the self-awareness to which his companions were first drawn in university.

Once that connection was established, it drove his determination. Loyola and his companions vowed to help people and to "find God in all things," and their loyalty and commitment to the cause is what attracted the attention of the Pope. With no long-term plan in place, no real established organization, and no name recognition, Loyola and his small group of friends had piqued the interest of the most esteemed man in the Catholic Church.

Once established, the Jesuits sought to help others discover their own self-awareness and deepen their relationship with God, often praising the practices illustrated in Loyola's *The Spiritual Exercises*, the book he had perfected since his time in Manresa. *The Spiritual Exercises* is composed of meditations, prayers, and contemplative practices that guide a thirty-day retreat of solitude and silence. Today the practice has been modified and considered "a retreat in daily life," adapted to the needs of the modern person. Although its roots are religious, the result is as much a deeper connection with oneself as it is with God.

The Jesuits believe their practices create the basis for future leaders, and their track record supports their notion. Instead of a "command and control" method, where one great person leads the rest, the Jesuit approach examines leadership through a very different prism, and leaders emerge in a very different light. Although not everyone can receive a Jesuit education, we can note the key differences in their leadership model, as follows:

- We're all leaders, and we're leading all the time, well or poorly.
- Leadership springs from within; it's about *who you are* as much as what you do.
- Leadership is not an act; it is a way of living.
- Leadership is never completed; it's an ongoing process.

With this model the Jesuits have found tremendous success, and while many organizations have weakened with age and changing environments, the Jesuits continue to thrive.

## Question to Ponder

From a hot-headed military man to superior general of one of the most renowned Catholic religious orders, Ignatius of Loyola's journey was unique, to say the least. His success reflects the importance of thorough self-awareness and understanding, as well as a thorough education.

The important question for you to ask is not, "Why me—why have I suffered in this life?" (That is a victim mentality.) Instead you should ask, "Why did I attract this hard hit in my life?" Reflect back to the important lessons you garnered from the hard hits you have suffered! Often these hard hits nudge you toward your purpose in life. It did for Ignatius, it did for me, and it can do it for you.

# 3
## HIS HIGHNESS PRINCE KARIM AGA KHAN IV
## EXEMPLARY BUSINESS, PHILANTHROPIC,
## AND SPIRITUAL LEADER

*"Spirituality should not become a way of escaping from the world
but rather a way of more actively engaging in it."*

—*Aga Khan IV*

I was raised in the Ismaili faith, a religion whose lineage spans over 1,400 years. The Aga Khan IV, the leader, or *imam*, of the Ismailis, has been my personal role model and guiding light throughout my life. Like all of those discussed in this book, he embodies satyagrahi leadership and is an accomplished social entrepreneur, a consummate philanthropist, and the spiritual leader of approximately twenty-five million Ismailis throughout the world.

One of the most significant gifts I have received from his guidance and my faith is the realization that spiritual life and material life are equally important. This has led me to never forsake my spiritual growth and evolution while still being able to focus on building my career and material life. I would not have been able to navigate the many challenges in my life without this important guidance. As I have said before, everyone will encounter problems that their intellect will not be able to resolve, or their hearts will not be able to heal, but there are *no* problems in life that your spirit cannot solve or heal. But to do that you have to have a strong spiritual foundation. The Aga Khan's omnipresent guidance has helped me build the spiritual foundation that has helped me navigate some of the direst challenges in my life, including losing Tariq.

Another important piece of advice he has given to me and the Ismailis living throughout the world is to embrace the citizenship of the country of our abode and respect the value and welfare of all subjects of our chosen countries, irrespective of race, religion, or socioeconomic status. The Aga Khan is a champion for promoting pluralism and civil society, believing that it is not enough to be diverse and tolerant of one another, but that we must actively seek an understanding across lines of differences. In his speech at the 2017 Global Pluralism Award ceremony in Ottawa, Canada, he said, "Some people make the mistake of thinking that pluralism requires them to dilute or de-emphasize their own distinctive identities. That's not true. What it requires is to ensure that one's individual identity is strong enough to engage confidently with those of other identities as we all walk together along the road to a better world."

Much of my work in the Tariq Khamisa Foundation, which I founded in 1995 in honor of my son, Tariq, is inspired by the Aga Khan's vision of creating a civil society. I am in deep gratitude for his enlightenment and for modeling these qualities in his own life. In 2017, I joined fifty thousand of his followers in Lisbon, Portugal, to celebrate his Diamond Jubilee, or sixtieth year of service. He continues to inspire me and millions of other Ismailis worldwide. He is indeed one of the brightest shining stars in the world and a moderate, compassionate, reasoning voice in the Islamic *Ummah* (community).

## An Introduction to the Ismaili Faith

The Shia Imami Ismaili Muslims, generally known as the Ismailis, belong to the Shia branch of Islam. The major split in Islam are the two branches referred to as Shias and Sunnis. Of course, like many other world religions, further sub-splits have occurred in both of these branches. Sunnis, however, at 87 percent of Islam, do form the majority. Approximately twenty million Ismailis live in over twenty-five different countries, mainly in Central and South Asia, the Indian Subcontinent, Africa, the Middle East, Europe, North America, and Australia. The Ismailis live in many Western and Eastern countries and are encouraged to strongly identify with the responsibilities of their adopted countries.

Throughout their fourteen hundred-year history, the Ismailis have been led by a living, hereditary imam. They trace the line of Imamat in hereditary succession from Ali, the cousin and son-in-law of Prophet Muhammad (may peace be upon him). The followers of Ali, or Shia, already in existence during the lifetime of the prophet, maintained that while the revelation ceased at the prophet's death, the community's need for spiritual and moral guidance continued.

They firmly believed that the legacy of Prophet Muhammad could be entrusted only to a member of his own family, in whom the prophet had invested his authority through designation before his death. That person was Ali, Prophet Muhammad's cousin and the husband of his daughter and only surviving child, Fatimah. The institution of Imamat was to continue thereafter on a hereditary basis, succession being based on designation by the imam of the time.

In time, the Shia were subdivided. The Ismailis gave their allegiance to Imam Ja'far as-Sadiq's eldest son, Ismail, from whom they derive their name. The Ismailis continue to believe in the line of Imamat in hereditary succession, continuing from Ismail to His Highness the Aga Khan, who is their present, forty-ninth imam in direct lineal descent from Prophet Muhammad.

The Ismaili interpretation is a major historical part of the faith of Islam, the Ismaili community being the second largest within the Shia branch of Islam. It has a creedal tradition, which stretches back to the early half of the seventh century, and a school of jurisprudence first promulgated more than a millennium ago, during the Ismaili Fatimid caliphate. The Ismaili Imamat is its institutional guide and leadership, and its multiple agencies are having an increasingly significant world impact.

The Ismailis are the only Shia Muslims to have a living, hereditary imam; it is the presence of the living imam that makes the community unique. Spiritual allegiance to the imam, and adherence to the Shia Imami Ismaili interpretation of Islam according to the guidance of the imam of the time, have engendered in the Ismaili community an ethos of self-reliance, unity, and a common identity. In a number of the countries where they live, the Ismailis have evolved a well-defined institutional framework through which they have, under the leadership and guidance of the imam, established schools, hospitals, health centers, housing societies, and a variety of social and economic development institutions for the common good of all citizens, regardless of their race or religion.

## Aga Khan IV—Prince Shah Karim Al Hussaini

The eldest son of Prince Aly Khan and his wife, Princess Tajuddawlah Aly Khan, Prince Karim Aga Khan was born December 13, 1936, in Geneva, Switzerland. He spent his childhood in Nairobi, Kenya, where he focused on his early education through private tutoring. He later attended the Institut Le Rosey in Switzerland, the most expensive boarding school in Europe, for nine years, though he states his grades were only "fair." Growing up, Prince Karim planned to study science at MIT, but his grandfather, Aga Khan III, did not allow it. As future leader of the Ismaili faith, Prince Karim was expected to learn all he could about the history and meaning behind his faith, as well as those related to it. He attended Harvard University, where he majored in oriental history to prepare him for his journey ahead.

In 1957 Prince Karim's grandfather passed away unexpectedly, leaving Prince Karim a huge role to fill. In his will, his grandfather stated that Prince Karim would succeed him, bypassing his father and uncle, who were in direct line to succession. Aga Khan III explained his rationale, stating, "I am convinced it is in the best interests of the Nizari Ismaili community that I should be succeeded by a young man who has been brought up and developed during recent years and in the midst of the new age, and who brings a new outlook on life to his office." His mention of the development of atomic science in his will led some Ismailis to refer to Prince Karim as the "Imam of the Atomic Age."

Only twenty and still a university student, Prince Karim's life changed overnight. He was now responsible for millions of other people. While finishing his last two years in college, Prince Karim was also hurriedly prepped for his role as successor. Although the late Aga Khan III had instructed that Prince Karim receive guidance from his widow, the Begum Aga Khan, for the first seven years of his Imamat, Aga Khan IV was determined to make his own mark on history. In 1959 he graduated from Harvard with a bachelor of arts degree in history with honors. The new Aga Khan IV was prepared to carry out his legacy.

Upon accepting the position of imam, Aga Khan IV planned to continue the work of his grandfather in building modern institutions to improve the quality of life of the Nizari Ismailis. During his first years as imam, the Aga Khan emphasized to his followers the importance of fostering positive relations with those of different ethnicities and religions—a highly appropriate message considering the racial tension between blacks and South Asians in East Africa at the time. He also promoted the need for material development, education, and confidence in religion. He encouraged the Nizari Ismailis to settle in the industrialized world in order to contribute toward the progress of communities in developing nations through various development programs.

In 1972 the power of the Aga Khan was tested when President Idi Amin of Uganda took power, ordering those of South Asian origin, including the Nizari Ismailis, to be expelled. South Asian families, some of whom had lived in Uganda for over one hundred years, were given ninety days to leave their homes and their country. Many had never left the country before and had nowhere to go.

Aga Khan IV was quick to act for the fate of those displaced. He phoned his long-time friend, Canadian Prime Minister Pierre Trudeau, and explained the situation. Trudeau's government agreed to allow thousands of Nizari Ismailis to immigrate to Canada. Communities were able to rebuild again, though thousands of miles from their mother homes, and still today Canada hosts a large and thriving Ismaili population. The efforts of the Aga Khan and host countries, as well as the material and moral support from Nizari Ismaili community programs, allowed hope to shine through a devastating situation. Many Ismailis resettled in European countries, including England, and in North America. Now one of the most important cultural centers of Ismailis worldwide, the Ismaili Centre is in London.

Because the Aga Khan puts a strong emphasis on caring for the spiritual, social, and physical needs of people in the local community, Ismailis have a strong bent toward volunteerism regardless of which country they live in. An Ismaili Constitution, created by the Aga Khan in 1986, governs the functioning of the diverse Ismaili communities residing across the globe. This creates a balance between a common set of principles shared by all Ismailis and a culture of contributing to the local community.

## Competency in His Field of Endeavor

The Aga Khan graduated with honors from Harvard University. He quickly took on the work of being the living imam of Ismaili Muslims even before graduating from college. Since the 1950s, the Aga Khan has proved to be an extremely successful businessperson, as well as leader of one of the world's largest philanthropies. A short list of accomplishments shows this success.

In 1960, he founded Nation Media Group, a Kenyan media company set up to provide independent voices in media (shortly before Ismailis and other Asians were required to leave Uganda). Since then, the company has expanded to include a number of Kiswahili and English national newspapers, a regional weekly, several radio and television stations, a strong online presence, and has diversified into magazines, directories, publishing, and courier services. It has become the region's leading media group in Uganda, Tanzania, and Rwanda. The Aga Khan has a passion for horse breeding and racing, which he has turned into one of the largest and most successful horse racing businesses globally. For decades he has invested in highly successful luxury hotels. Through these and other endeavors, he was named the ninth richest royal in the world. For many people, these material accomplishments might constitute the definition of success. But his material successes in business have a relatively minor impact when compared to the humanitarian work he promotes through the Aga Khan Development Network.

## Competency in Tackling Societal Issues

One only needs to look at the honors, honorary degrees, and awards received from dozens of foreign governments, colleges, and professional organizations to understand the reach, scale, and impact of Aga Khan's globally focused work through the Aga Khan Development Network (AKDN). The ethical principles of the AKDN promote the "social conscience of Islam through institutional action," resulting in agency work that can "help relieve society of ignorance, disease and deprivation," according to the Institute of Ismaili Studies.

It is the mission of the AKDN to support human development, embodying as much of heaven on earth as possible. Structurally, the AKDN is a group of private, nondenominational development agencies that work primarily in the poorest parts of Asia and Africa with communities that are primarily Ismaili or have a large minority Ismaili community. But the agencies work to improve the living conditions and opportunities for the poor regardless of religion, race, gender, or other demographics. The AKDN operates in thirty countries around the world and employs over eighty thousand paid staff, mostly in developing countries. While the agencies are secular, they are guided by Islamic ethics, which bridge faith and society. The Aga Khan and AKDN work toward a common goal—to build institutions and programs that can respond to the challenges of social, economic, and cultural change on an ongoing basis. The AKDN works in close partnership with public and private institutions, including, among others, governments, international organizations, companies, foundations, and universities. It is now one of the largest development networks in the world.

In terms of the practical consequences of this development work, millions of people have benefitted from support through AKDN and its partners. Annually, the AKDN helps over eight million people achieve greater food security and quality of life, gives five million people access to quality healthcare, generates electricity for ten million people, and gives education services for two million students.

In addition, Aga Khan IV established the Aga Khan Award for Architecture and the promotion of Islamic architecture in cooperation with Harvard University and the Massachusetts Institute of Technology (MIT). The award is given on a triennial basis and has supported diverse projects across the globe, including innovative designs for parks, bridges, surgery centers, public policy institutes, mosques, and college campus buildings. It is one of the most prestigious architectural awards in the world.

## Competency in Spirit

The Aga Khan IV is understood by Ismaili Muslims to be a descendant of the Prophet Muhammad and the living imam who promotes a healthy and virtuous Islamic way of life for Ismaili followers. Upon receiving the Tutzing Award for Tolerance in 2006, Aga Khan IV said that "spirituality should not become a way of escaping from the world but rather a way of more actively engaging in it." Related to social issues, self-realization is not an end in itself. It is directed toward social justice, helping others materially and therefore spiritually. Personal competency in spirit bridges relationships between self and other.

In Islam, *din* and *dunya* refer to the spiritual realm and the material realm, respectively. Each human being is a "vicegerent of God," and this has ultimate value. Everyday life can and should be a field for spiritual realization; a divine balance between the mundane and ephemeral is sought. The AKDN's many programs demonstrate this commitment in the everyday realm, where compassion, tolerance, mutual aid, knowledge and clarity of mind, respect for life, self-reliance, and other positive traits are developed.

## Question to Ponder

The tendency in the West is to be overly spiritual or overly materialistic. While we are spiritual beings in a human form, we are also humans in a spiritual form. Both of these manifestations have responsibilities, and it is important to fulfill both of them.

The question that you need to ponder is, "Does my lifestyle put equal emphasis on my material life and spiritual life?" It does not mean that you need to spend forty hours a week or eight hours a day on both, but it does mean that you need to have a daily spiritual practice. My own method is to meditate two hours a day. I meditate three different times a day and do a different practice each of these three different times. I have created my own meditation technology, and it is a free download from my website www.azimkhamisa.com. If you scroll down to the bottom left side of my Home page, you will see a preamble that explains my methodology and two separate guided meditations: one is on forgiveness, and the other is on manifesting your goals. Almost all of my aha's, ideas, books, and answers come from my meditations. For two hours a day I am not living in my head but with my spirit that provides wisdom, guidance, and answers. All the answers you seek live within you—the question is, are you tapping into your soul every day? If not, I recommend a daily spiritual practice; I never skip meditating—it has been my mainstay for most of my life.

# 4
## MATA AMRITANANDAMAYI (AMMA)
## THE HUGGING SAINT

*"Most people are concerned only with what they can get from the world,
but it is what we are able to give to others that
determines the quality of our life."*

—*Amma*

Mata Amritanandamayi—better known simply as Amma—was born in a remote coastal village in South India. As a child she was exposed to the poverty that existed within her community and beyond, and she often offered clothes and food from her own home to those on the streets. Though her parents scolded her generosity, Amma moved forward with confidence in her life of service and compassionate care for all beings, enveloping in a motherly embrace each person who sought her solace. With just a grade school education, Amma has accomplished what government officials and foreign diplomats could not: she organized disaster relief after the 2004 tsunami when government efforts were inadequate, she has led sanitation efforts on the banks of the Ganges river, she has established hospitals in India led by volunteer foreign doctors to assist those who cannot pay for treatment, and much, much more.

Given the name Sudhamani Idamannel, Amma was born September 27, 1953, into a low-caste family residing in the fishing village of Parayakadavu, India. From the moment Sudhamani was born, she was considered an eccentric child—it was said her skin was dark blue, and she did not cry, but smiled.

Although her skin eventually changed to a brown much darker than that of the other children in her village, Sudhamani grew with the smile she had possessed since birth. She had a strong devotional element to her Hindu faith—it is said that by the age of five she was spending much of her time singing devotional prayers, many toward Lord Krishna, the Hindu god of compassion, tenderness, and love.

Sudhamani also cultivated her generous, compassionate nature at a young age, which was not always appreciated by her parents. When Sudhamani was nine, her mother became very ill. Although she excelled in school, she had to cut her education short to take care of her entire family. With seven brothers and sisters to feed, the task consumed her day and night. As part of her chores, Sudhamani gathered food scraps from neighbors to feed her family's goats and cows. But as she traveled from house to house, Sudhamani was confronted with the intense poverty and suffering of those even less fortunate than her poor family. She was often scolded for bringing food from her home to share with those of the untouchable class—people whose occupations and habits involved ritually polluting activities, such as butchers or those who disposed of dead animals. These people were ostracized by the rest of society and often left to live in squalor.

According to Hinduism, the suffering of an individual is due to his or her own *karma*—the results of actions done in the past. Amma understood and respected karma, but she believed it was no excuse for inaction. I once visited her ashram in Kerala, India, where I met her and spoke at her university. Contemplating the principle of karma, I heard her ask, "If it is one man's karma to suffer, isn't it our *dharma* (duty) to help ease his suffering and pain?"

Sudhamani gave food her family could not afford to give and whatever valuables she could find in her home to be sold to help those who needed it. Despite their caste level, she embraced each person she encountered in a warm, nurturing hug, earning her the name Amma, or "Mother." Amma's hugs became her signature form of giving *darshan*. In the Hindu religion, *darshan* means "to see," and traditionally a master is seen but never touched. Amma's darshan is unique in that she does the exact opposite of what is expected of her as a spiritual leader. When asked in one of her many interviews about her desire to embrace every person who comes to her for solace, she responded, "I don't see if it is a man or a woman. I don't see anyone different from my own self. A continuous stream of love flows from me to all of creation. This is my inborn nature. The duty of a doctor is to treat patients. In the same way, my duty is to console those who are suffering." Her parents were furious and embarrassed by Amma's interactions with the untouchables. In India women were expected to be silent, to melt into the background with their only duties being to serve their family, husband, and children. But Amma continued to bring the controversial issue of caste and poverty to light, feeding, clothing, assisting, and hugging every person who sought her comfort. She persisted despite punishment from her parents and society's disapproval, smiling all the while.

As a young woman, Amma was said to already have begun performing miracles—kissing cobras, diverting rainstorms, and feeding more than a thousand people from a single small pot. Her days were spent serving her family and community, her nights with intense meditation. To cure her of what her parents considered "madness," Amma was sent to a relative's house, where she was kept busy with constant work. When that did not distract her from her spiritual conquests, her parents tried to marry her off. But Amma had already begun placing the pieces of her life-to-be, one that did not involve the roles of wife and mother. By the time she reached her early twenties, Amma had established an inner bliss and was believed to be connected with Lord Krishna, whom she had admired and worshiped most throughout her childhood. Her mystical experiences intensified, and she began to attract followers who felt something profound within her. Spiritual seekers began to reside at her parents' property in Parayakadavu in the hopes of becoming her disciples. This small group formed the nucleus of Amma's own informal ashram. Despite her motherly nature, Amma gave strict instructions to her disciples in hopes of leading them toward their own enlightenment, including rising at 4:30 every morning and spending a set amount of time in meditation; *kirtan*, or religious chanting and storytelling; and selfless service. Amma recognized the possibilities presented with her new leadership position—with the number of people rallying to join her cause, she soon set her sights on making a significant impact on the well-being of Indian society and the world.

Amma established the Mata Amritanandamayi Math (MAM) in 1981, an international charitable organization aimed at the spiritual and material upliftment of humankind. MAM began as a few thatched-roof cottages on her parents' property, tackling immediate problems in the surrounding community such as poverty and homelessness. As word of Amma's selflessness spread throughout India, many more people joined in her efforts, developing one of the most sophisticated and respected nonprofits in the world.

With the help of those who share her vision, Amma is able to feed more than ten million people every year throughout India and another million in other impoverished countries, run homes for the elderly (now four in total), two care homes for children, two of the most advanced hospitals in India, an extensive educational system for the underprivileged and disadvantaged sections of society, and MAM's own university, Amrita Vishwa Vidyapeetham. As of 2011, MAM has constructed more than forty thousand homes for the homeless in an effort to renovate India's slum areas, complete with new roads, sewer systems, town halls, wells, and electricity. Many believe Amma is shouldering the burden of the state government in the development of the downtrodden and poor.

In the wake of the Gujarat earthquake of 2001—the 7.7-magnitude quake that killed between thirteen thousand and twenty-three thousand people and destroyed four hundred thousand homes—Amma's response to reach out to those in need was as natural as it had been for her as a little girl. It took the government of Kerala five days to merely announce what it would do in the way of aid, while Amma had organized a response effort within hours, sending doctors, ambulances, and hordes of volunteers to the region, setting up shelters, providing medical aid, and cleaning up the carnage of the homes and villages destroyed. When the initial horror had subsided and many relief groups had left Gujarat, MAM continued to rebuild three villages, constructing twelve hundred earthquake-proof homes, medical clinics, schools, water tanks, community centers, temples, and Jamat Khanas. Although Amma could not completely soothe the pain of losing a home, a business, an entire community, and so many loved ones, she and the volunteers of MAM helped provide a new beginning for more than sixty-five hundred citizens of Gujarat.

Since then, MAM has assisted in the disaster relief of the Kumbakonam fire of 2004, helping console the friends and family of the ninety-two children killed and eighteen severely injured when their nursery school caught fire; the Indian Ocean tsunami of 2004, working to improve every aspect of the survivors' lives in one of the most multifaceted, comprehensive, and sustained disaster-relief projects ever undertaken by a nongovernmental agency; the Mumbai flood of 2005, distributing essentials such as food, clean water, and mats, as well as helping rebuild villages and towns swept away during the four-day rain; Hurricane Katrina of 2005, helping clear debris and feeding and sheltering refugees; the Kashmir earthquake of 2005, aiding more than five hundred thousand families who had been affected by the 7.6-magnitude quake; and the Karnataka flood of 2013 and the Jammu and Kashmir floods of 2014, both of which the MAM continues to assist in the rebuilding of homes and villages, as well as the rehabilitation of those affected.

With the disaster relief Amma offered came the revelation that at least one member in each family should engage in a profession that was not reliant on unforeseeable weather patterns. In most cases, not only had homes and lives been destroyed by natural disasters, but the environment had been affected as well, devastating farmers and fishermen and hindering their progress toward healing. In 2006 MAM launched the Amrita Self Reliance Education and Employment (SREE) program, the Ashram's first community-based, self-help program. The program facilitates training in tailoring, nursing, driving, education, handicrafts, and electronic repair. The program also aims to help empower women, equipping those unemployed or economically vulnerable with the skills and means to start up small-scale, cottage-industry businesses. As of 2011, thirty-five hundred of these self-help groups have received microcredit loans to expand their business, benefitting more than sixty thousand families.

In 2005, in recognition of its outstanding disaster relief efforts and other humanitarian work, the United Nations granted MAM special consultative status with its economic and social council, enabling collaboration with UN agencies. Today, Amma runs a large network of global charities, known as Embracing the World. Her most recent goals for her network include the elimination of human trafficking and slavery by the year 2020, a commitment organized by the Global Freedom Network in 2014, signed and shared by other major religious leaders worldwide. She's also working with the scientific community to develop ways to alleviate suffering through technological research, such as a landslide detection system.

Amma often travels to spread her message of unconditional love and compassion throughout the world. From migrant workers to Hollywood celebrities, tens of thousands of fans and devotees await her arrival on her international tours, hoping to receive one of her revered hugs that her admirers describe as "an infusion of pure, unconditional love that works on you like an elixir, cleansing the soul and bringing about a higher state of consciousness." Throughout her life it is believed that Amma has embraced more than thirty-four million people, and she shows no sign of stopping. Of her tireless devotion to service, she states, "The lifespan of a butterfly is only a few days to a week. Yet how joyously it flies around! It spreads delight and happiness to everyone. Our lives should be like this."

## Competency in Her Field of Endeavor

Amma was born into a poor family in a small remote village, far away from any progressive cities or organizations that could appreciate what many would consider radical ideas in 1950s India. Besides her short stint in elementary school, Amma did not receive any sort of formal education, nor has she ever had any sort of established "career." But Amma has been successful in everything she has ever sought to do—if her career title were leader, mother, inspirer, or entrepreneur, she'd be one of the world's most prosperous. As a child, she believed her vocation was to help those in need, to the best of her abilities; with no money or support from her family, Amma relied on her spirit to guide her, inspiring those around her with her generosity and selflessness. Soon, doctors and caregivers from around the world, teachers and professors, philanthropists, politicians, world leaders, scientists, and thousands upon thousands of volunteers rallied to support Amma and MAM, many volunteering at her hospitals, caregiver homes, universities, educational organizations, orphanages, soup kitchens, and renovation sites without pay. Her organization raises about $20 million per year from donors worldwide, impressed that Amma appears to accomplish what politicians simply cannot. Her heart has no limits; she sets her mind to a task and sees that it is done. Driven purely on passion, perseverance, and faith, Amma has developed an organization that arguably has done more in terms of humanitarian aid than India's own government. From nothing, she has built an empire of compassion, earning her name "Amma, mother to all."

In addition to her success in humanitarian aid, Amma has also become a world-renowned spiritual leader. Her tiny ashram of a few thatched roof huts has blossomed into a small metropolis, home to thirty-five hundred monastic disciples complete with its own university, dormitories, restaurants, and temples. But Amma doesn't spend much time at her ashram; throughout most of the year she travels the globe to raise money for her organization and to promote her Hindu philosophy emphasizing love, introspection, and selflessness, often including up to twenty-two hour hugging sessions for the thousands who wish to experience her darshan. Her message is not restricted to fellow Hindus; she states that her religion is love. She has never asked anyone to change their religion but only to contemplate the essential principles of their own faith or values and to try to live accordingly. Amma's patience, all-inclusiveness, wisdom, and earthy humor have attracted a wide spectrum of followers, more than a million strong.

## Competency in Tackling Societal Issues

Before she could even understand social classes, caste systems, and the relationships between the haves and the have-nots, Amma recognized her duty to serve. Perhaps it was her strong Hindu faith, or maybe the nondiscriminatory and unsullied compassion of a child wanting to help; regardless, the pull Amma felt toward aiding her fellow humans was not only powerful but infectious.

Amma runs one of the most successful humanitarian nonprofits in the world, its goal to alleviate suffering wherever and however it is needed. But what makes MAM so unique is its volunteers' willingness to respect and understand those they are helping and to go above and beyond what is immediately needed of them. For example, after the Indian Ocean tsunami of 2004, many people affected said their lives were actually better after the disaster because of MAM's dedication to assist even after the carnage had been cleared away. The organization not only had set up a new path for survivors but guided them down that path, offering job training for those who had never received a formal education, housing with plumbing and electricity, and schools for children whose futures would otherwise have consisted of hard labor. Amma sets her sights above mere aid—she truly aims to better the lives of everyone she touches.

## Competency in Spirit

Despite her family's harsh punishment and society's disapproval of her actions early on, Amma never let any force create a barrier between herself and her purpose. But Amma was not driven by the promise of money, fame, or success—she sought spiritual fulfillment, not only within herself but within those who chose to follow her example of selfless service. With spiritual fulfillment came peace, happiness, and contentment, as well as material prosperity. But Amma seems to have been born with a strong connection to spirit—some even consider her a reincarnation of the Hindu god Lord Krishna. But Amma believes anyone can experience the same blissful divine consciousness she has discovered within herself, despite life's tribulations and impediments.

## The Five Competencies for Enlightened Leadership

Amma has developed a formula to set the pace toward spiritual fulfillment and enlightened leadership, known as the "mirror model" among her disciples. The techniques she describes are neither revolutionary nor unique, but, used in conjunction with one another, they can dramatically alter the mind-set of any individual, especially those who find themselves consumed with selfish desires and material success. The five tools of the mirror model are as follows:

1. Meditation

Sometimes we may find ourselves overwhelmed, lost in our ways, or torn between an issue among friends, family, team members, etc. Successful leaders need to consider every direction of an issue, every solution, and every outcome—meditation focuses on finding the silence within and transmitting that into action, allowing one to give guidance and direction without losing clarity, patience, and composure. Meditation seems to intimidate many people because of the belief that it requires too much time and an outcome that is not always promised. But meditation time is determined by an individual—it can be as short as half an hour a day. But once given a fair shot, those who choose to meditate find invaluable their inner capacity to let go, withdraw, and remain aloof in order to contemplate our concerns and those of others until the shell of the solution breaks.

2. Intuition

Once we realize the importance of meditation, we begin to develop another faculty, an intuitive mind that guides us toward the right decision, the right time, and the right understanding. Moments are frequent when our intellect cannot provide the answers we seek, when we become stuck researching and contemplating an issue too abstract. This is when we need the help of intuition, a connection with an unknown source of knowledge masked by our intellect and emotions—an inner voice that always has your best interests at heart. Amma states,

"To be intuitive means to be spontaneous. The first step toward being spontaneous is effort and hard work. The second step is to let go, forget all that you have done, and be in the present, in a restful state of mind. From that restfulness emerges the third step, and the intuitive mind begins to function."

3. Responding Rather than Reacting

When confronted with new and unfamiliar situations or with meeting new people, we may approach one of two ways—responding or reacting. Response is a natural and relaxed state of mind, more open and accepting of new situations. Responding people are more understanding and sympathetic, considering situations with a nonjudgmental attitude.

On the other hand, reactive people are more prone to letting their emotions run the situation. Reactive people are easily upset or agitated, often losing their calm and allowing their decisions to lack precision. They tend to assess a situation without considering the implications of all sides, so the outcome is often that of a narrow mind.

With conscious decision-making, anyone can respond rather than react. But it can go against our natural rationale. We often view people, situations, and objects in light of our past experiences—we can't help but be judgmental; it happens unconsciously. But when we judge something, we are reacting from the past, not responding to the present. Our impressions of the world around us are like a cloud of smoke veiling what *was* from what *is*. Is it safe to say that you are not the same person you were ten years ago? Or you are not the same person you were yesterday? Everything is continually shifting, taking a new shape, and becoming new—but when people view with a mind fixed in the past, they do not see the fresh aspect of life. To summarize, the majority of people believe they are responding, when in fact they are reacting—it's second nature to view situations from our past memories.

The best way to combat reaction is to delay the response—to really stop and think about what you are planning to say or do, and what the possible outcomes of your solution may be. Amma suggests:

"When someone criticizes you, at least tell the other person, 'Let me sleep on it, and I will come back to you in a few hours. If what you said is true, I will accept it. Or else I will give it back to you.' Most probably, you will realize that the other person was right and you were wrong because you were in a reactive mode, and he was in a calmer state of mind and could step aside and be witness."

For every emotional disturbance there is a certain recovery time, allowing a rise in our awareness level. This is where meditation comes in to play—we need time to silence our minds and reflect on ourselves, our actions and decisions. When we keep working on these awareness levels, the delay before the response becomes shorter and shorter. Eventually, we will be able to maintain calmness and confidence at all times, allowing our thought process to become much sharper and our decisions more accurate.

4. Oneness

It is of the utmost importance that every leader possess a sense of oneness between themselves and their followers through love and the power of listening. "Love and listening" are one and the same—a loving heart listens.

When one feels they are truly listened to, they gain strength and the courage to open up, trust, and perform their duties not just out of the promise of monetary compensation but a sense of dedication. When team members understand and empathize with one another, activities synch with that of the other and the entire team can work together toward the target goals. Amma uses the metaphor of electricity powering a fridge, a lamp, and a TV to describe the same life principle that connects every person to one another. She states, "In a similar manner, we are not totally disconnected entities, living in an isolated world; we are all part and parcel of the universal chain."

    5.  Reverence

With oneness comes reverence, the respect and acceptance of every person regardless of differences. A workplace built upon reverence will have employees who love and respect their employer, and vice versa, creating a comparatively friction-free working atmosphere.

Reverence, however, can be difficult to achieve, as we are not often exposed to cultures outside our own. Classes on cultural diversity and values are seldom offered before college, and by that time students may not find the importance in it. But as the world becomes more globalized, every career is beginning to stress the importance of cultural understanding and international protocol. It is fair to say that every culture values love, compassion, and respect, and every person should be treated accordingly. Amma spoke of her reverence during her speech at the United Nations Alliance of Civilization Conference in 2012:

"In my experience, the one language that humanity and all other living beings understand is love. For the past forty years, I have been communicating with people of all languages, races, colors, castes, and religions, from the very poorest to the rich and famous through the language of love. There are no barriers for love. I have full faith in the transformational power of love to unite all hearts."

With these five tools, one can work to become a leader grounded in compassion, respect, and understanding. These qualities, along with a strong dedication to serving one's fellow beings, will help guide one toward spiritual connection and fulfillment. Once a relationship with the spirit is formed, one will be able to follow whatever path they have chosen with confidence and reassurance.

Amma, once a poor Indian girl from a rural fishing village, has constructed one of the most respected humanitarian efforts in the world. With her enduring spirit, charisma, and dedication to assist, she has inspired millions to help serve humanity. If there is one thing to be learned from Amma, it's that people are not always inspired by money or promises of fame and power. Sometimes it just takes a vision and the dedication to pursue with all your heart to inspire people to follow.

## Question to Ponder

Here the important question to ponder is, "Am I spending all my time in my head and solving all my challenges with intellect?" The truth is, intellect by itself is not a reliable faculty. A good friend of mine says, "A mind is a dangerous place to go by yourself." Because the mind will justify anything. Hitler killed six million Jews—he did not do the killing; the killing was done by MDs and PhDs who had taken an oath never to take a life. Even Einstein, the preeminent intellect of the last century and this century, taught, "We should take care not to make the intellect our God; it has, of course, powerful muscles, but no personality. It cannot lead, it can only serve." So faith is an important faculty to develop if you are going to be able to manifest what seems impossible. Look what Amma has accomplished from faith. She routinely visits the USA, and people line up for hours to get a hug from her. I just got my fourth hug from her last month. Another question to ponder is, "How strong is your faith?"

# 5
## ELIE WIESEL
## BREAKING THE SILENCE

*"Mankind must remember that peace is not God's gift
to his creatures, it is our gift to each other."*
—*Elie Wiesel*

Elie Wiesel was a Romanian-born writer, professor, political activist, Nobel Laureate, and Holocaust survivor. From his own humiliating and terrifying experience in Hitler's death camps during World War II, Wiesel dedicated his life to defending human rights across the globe. He helped establish the United States Holocaust Memorial Museum in Washington, DC, and has campaigned for victims of oppression in places like South Africa, Nicaragua, Kosovo, and Sudan. After he was awarded the Nobel Peace Prize in 1986, Wiesel founded the Elie Wiesel Foundation for Humanity.

Eliezer "Elie" Wiesel was born September 30, 1928, in Sighet (now Sighetu Marmatiei), Romania, the third of four children and the only son to Sarah Feig and Shlomo Wiesel. Growing up in a small mountain village, Wiesel's world revolved around family, religious study, community, and God. His mother was the daughter of a well-respected farmer, while his father owned a grocery store in town. Most of the time his family spoke Yiddish, the historical language of the Ashkenazi Jews, but he also learned German, Hungarian, and Romanian. His father felt it important to instill a strong sense of humanism within his son and encouraged him to read modern Hebrew literature, as well as study Hebrew and the Torah, as requested by his mother. Wiesel has said his father represented reason, while his mother represented faith, both powerful values evident from his lineage.

In 1944, when Wiesel was fifteen years old, World War II had ravaged much of Europe. The Nazis soon made their way to Wiesel's city, ending his idyllic life. He and his family, along with the rest of the town's Jewish population, were forced into one of the two confinement ghettos set up in Sighet. The town where he was born and raised had become his prison, the buildings and familiar faces once so commonplace now shrouded in confusion and despair. In his essay "This I Believe," he said, "I remember, May 1944: I was 15-and-a-half, and I was thrown into a haunted universe where the story of the human adventure seemed to swing irrevocably between horror and malediction." You can listen to him read the rest of the essay in the archives of the radio program *All Things Considered* on NPR.org.

A few weeks after being relocated to the ghetto, the Hungarian authorities, under German pressure, began to deport the Jewish population to Auschwitz concentration camp, where more than 90 percent of the people were exterminated upon arrival. Immediately after the Wiesel family had arrived there, his mother and younger sister were among those murdered. In his book *Night*, Wiesel writes of his first experience at Auschwitz:

"Never shall I forget that night, the first night in camp, that turned my life into one long night seven times sealed. Never shall I forget that smoke. Never shall I forget the small faces of the children whose bodies I saw transformed into smoke under a silent sky. Never shall I forget those flames that consumed my faith forever. Never shall I forget the nocturnal silence that deprived me for all eternity the desire to live. Never shall I forget those moments that murdered my God and my soul and turned my dreams to ashes. Never shall I forget these things, even if I am condemned to live as long as God himself. Never."

Separated from his two other sisters, Wiesel and his father were later deported to the concentration camp in Buchenwald, where inmate number "A-7713" was tattooed on his left arm. Until that transfer, Wiesel admitted his primary motivation for trying to survive was knowing his father was still alive: "I knew that if I died, he would die." Through extreme hunger and thirst, constant beatings, numerous "selections" to eliminate the weaker men, and nights spent in the harshest winter conditions with little more than a soggy blanket, Wiesel and his father fought to keep each other alive. Unfortunately, Wiesel's efforts were in vain; his father died before the camp was liberated, leaving Wiesel an orphan at sixteen years old.

On April 11, 1945, the Buchenwald concentration camp was liberated by the US Third Army, freeing Wiesel and some twenty thousand prisoners. By the end of the war, the Nazis were responsible for more than eleven million deaths over the span of four years, six million of which were of Jewish descent.

Wiesel joined a transport of one thousand child survivors of Buchenwald to Écouis, France, where the French Children's Aid Society had set up a rehabilitation center. Wiesel was placed with a smaller group of ninety to one hundred boys from orthodox homes who wanted kosher facilities and a higher level of religious observance. They were cared for in a home in Ambloy under the directorship of Judith Hemmendinger, a German-born Israeli researcher and author who worked with child survivors of the Holocaust. The house was subsequently moved to Taverny and operated until 1947, when the last of the boys had found a permanent placement.

After the last couple of years in the home, Wiesel traveled to Paris, where he learned French and studied literature, philosophy, and psychology at the Sorbonne, the historical house of the former University of Paris. By the time he was nineteen, he had begun working as a journalist, writing in French, while also teaching Hebrew and working as a choirmaster. In 1949 he traveled to Israel as a correspondent for the French newspaper *L'Arche,* where he was then hired as the roaming international correspondent for the Israeli newspaper *Yedioth Ahronoth.*

Despite Wiesel's success as a journalist, for ten years after the war he refused to write about or discuss his experiences during the Holocaust. Those who had survived the war did not want to relive their pain; they did not speak of their past, not even to their own children. Many wanted to go about their lives as if the atrocities had never happened. But Wiesel began to reconsider his decision after meeting with French author François Mauriac, the 1952 Nobel Laureate in Literature, who eventually became Wiesel's close friend. Mauriac persuaded him to go against the wall of silence and begin the difficult task of sharing his story. Wiesel resolved to begin writing of his trials during the war. Years later, after learning he had won the Nobel Prize for his efforts, he explained in a press conference at 92nd Street Y in New York City, "I decided to devote my life to telling the story because I felt that, having survived, I owe something to the dead. And anyone who does not remember betrays them again."

Wiesel re-immersed himself into that harrowing period he had tried so long not to revisit. But writing, the one thing that came so naturally to him, proved difficult when trying to find the right words to describe his most dehumanizing moments. "While I had many things to say," he wrote in the preface to his book *Night*, "I did not have the words to say them. . . . how was one to rehabilitate and transform words betrayed and perverted by the enemy? Hunger—thirst—fear—transport—selection—fire—chimney. . . . I would pause at every sentence and start over and over again. I would conjure up other verbs, other images, other silent cries. It was still not right."

Eventually Wiesel did finish his nine-hundred-page memoir, *Un di velt hot geshvign* (*And the World Remained Silent*), in Yiddish, which was then condensed to a little more than one hundred pages. But despite shortening his story to appeal more to publishers, all the major publishing houses turned the book down. They wanted to promote more "optimistic" books, not be reminded of what they had allowed to occur. Yet none of this appeared to have diminished Wiesel's persistence. His condensed manuscript, *La Nuit*, or *Night*, was eventually published in French in 1955. The English translation followed five years later in 1960. The book sold few copies after its initial release but still attracted interest from reviewers, arguing that no single work did so much to lift the silence that had enveloped survivors and bring forth what had occurred in the "Kingdom of Night." Readership began to grow, at first gradually and then exponentially. *Night* was eventually translated into thirty languages with ten million copies sold in the United States.

In 1955, Wiesel moved to New York as foreign correspondent for the Israel daily, *Yedioth Ahronoth*, where he met his wife, Marion Erster Rose. The two married in 1969 and had one son, Shlomo Elisha Wiesel, named after Wiesel's father.

In the United States Wiesel went on to write over forty books, most of them nonfiction Holocaust literature, and novels. He has been awarded a number of literary prizes and is considered among the most important authors in describing the Holocaust from a highly personal perspective. Some historians credit Wiesel with giving the term "Holocaust" its present meaning, though he never felt the word could adequately describe that dark period in human history.

After achieving success and notoriety as a writer, Wiesel and his wife, Marion, established the Elie Wiesel Foundation for Humanity in 1986, using the money he had received from being awarded the Nobel Peace Prize that same year to fund the organization. The foundation's mission statement, created in remembrance of the Holocaust, is "to combat indifference, intolerance, and injustice through international dialogue and youth-focused programs that promote acceptance, understanding and equality." Wiesel has dedicated the foundation to bringing people together from all over the world to share ideas on political, cultural, religious, and academic boundaries.

Since its establishment the foundation has opened up two Beit Tzipora Centers in Israel for Ethiopian-Jewish refugees. The centers were founded in the mid-90s following the rescue of thousands of Ethiopian Jews from Africa, where they were facing persecution and violence. The idea for these centers came to the Elie Wiesel Foundation after witnessing the growing need for safe and educational centers for the Ethiopian-Jewish refugees in Israel. Together the two locations provide more than one thousand children with after-school programs, encouraging them to be knowledgeable and participate fully in society. A similar center was also established in Tel Aviv during the 2007 refugee crisis in Darfur, which provided children with English and Hebrew training, computer technology education, tutoring, arts and crafts, and, most importantly, counseling. While he was still alive, Elie and his wife were extremely involved with the centers and frequently made trips to provide encouragement to the children.

Wiesel's passion for education and teaching gained him the position of Andrew W. Mellon Professor of the Humanities at Boston University in 1976, where he taught in both its religion and philosophy departments. The university created the Elie Wiesel Center for Jewish Studies in his honor. Before then he had been a Distinguished Professor at the City University of New York and a member of the American Federation of Teachers. Wiesel would go on to teach courses and lectures at a number of universities, including Yale and Columbia.

Elie Wiesel also served as chairman of the Presidential Commission on the Holocaust (later renamed the United States Holocaust Memorial Council) from 1978 to 1986, spearheading the construction of the United States Holocaust Memorial Museum (USHMM) in Washington, DC. Since its dedication on April 22, 1993, the Museum has had nearly forty million visitors, including more than ten million school children, ninety-nine heads of state, and more than thirty-five hundred foreign officials from over 211 countries. The USHMM's collection contains historical artifacts, including a haunting collection of shoes left behind by victims of the execution chambers, archival footage, library items, and a list of the two hundred thousand registered survivors of the concentration camps. Researchers at the museum have documented forty-two thousand five hundred ghettos and concentration camps erected by the Nazis throughout German-controlled Europe from 1933–1945.

The museum also features a Hall of Remembrance, the USHMM's official memorial to the victims and survivors of the Holocaust. Visitors can memorialize the event by lighting candles, visiting the eternal flame, and reflecting in silence in the hexagonal hall.

In 1986 Wiesel was awarded the Nobel Peace Prize for speaking out against violence, repression, and racism. Wiesel delivered his acceptance speech as a call to action:

"Silence encourages the tormentor, never the tormented. Sometimes we must interfere. When human lives are endangered, when human dignity is in jeopardy, national borders and sensitivities become irrelevant."

Wiesel received many other prizes for his work against injustice, including the Congressional Gold Medal in 1985 and the Presidential Medal of Freedom. He and I are both featured in the 2007 documentary *The Power of Forgiveness*, directed by Martin Doblmeier.

Although he was seen as a dominant speaker on the subject of the Holocaust, as a political activist Wiesel also advocated for many other causes, including the Israeli conflict, the plight of Soviet and Ethiopian Jews, and the Bosnian victims of genocide. In April 1999 he delivered the speech "The Perils of Indifference" in Washington, DC, criticizing the people and countries who chose to be indifferent while the Holocaust was occurring. He defined indifference as being neutral between two sides, which ultimately amounted to overlooking the victims of the Holocaust. Throughout his speech he expressed the view that even a little bit of attention, positive or negative, was better than no attention at all. He said:

"The opposite of love is not hatred, it's indifference. . . . Even hatred at times may elicit a response. You fight it. You denounce it. You disarm it. Indifference elicits no response. Indifference is not a response. Indifference is not a beginning; it is an end."

"The Perils of Indifference" is noted as one of the most influential speeches of all time, and Wiesel kept to its example. In 2003 he discovered and publicized the fact that at least two hundred eighty thousand Romanian and Ukrainian Jews had been massacred in Romanian-run death camps. In 2006 he appeared before the UN Security Council to call attention to the humanitarian crisis in Darfur. In 2007 the Elie Wiesel Foundation for Humanity issued a letter condemning Armenian genocide denial, a letter that was signed by fifty-three Nobel laureates who considered Turkey's ninety-year campaign to downplay its actions during the genocide a double killing. He was also active in trying to prevent Iran from making nuclear weapons, and condemned Hamas for the "use of children as human shields" during the 2014 Israel-Gaza conflict by running an ad in several large newspapers. The *Times* refused to run the advertisement, stating, "The opinion expressed is too strong, and too forcefully made, and would cause concern amongst a significant number of *Times* readers." The man who was once so haunted by his experience that he kept his story silent for ten years had become one of the world's most outspoken allies against injustice.

On July 2, 2016, Elie Wiesel passed away at his home in Manhattan. He was eighty-seven years old.

Elie Wiesel possessed an enormous will to fight his entire life—for his and his father's survival during the unimaginable terrors of the Holocaust, and for the lives of thousands around the world experiencing a terror of their own. He was a warrior against silence, against indifference, and he made sure his voice was heard and responses were elicited. New leaders of our generation must not disregard the issues our world faces, though they may not be at our doorstep. New leaders have a responsibility to learn from the traumatic and shameful events of our history, and to make an earnest effort to never let these things happen again.

## Competency in His Field of Endeavor

Survivor, journalist, writer, political activist—Wiesel's many titles have ultimately tied into his lifelong fight against oppression and injustice.

As a child who had already experienced the terrors of Nazi Germany, it is not surprising Wiesel channeled his writing toward journalism. A journalist has the responsibility to uncover the truths hidden away from society and bring those truths to light. Investigative journalists are often referred to as "watchdogs," using their influence to keep others in line or else expose them to the public. But today many news sources lack integrity and spread fake or biased news. Without a reputable third party to watch the watchdogs, a free media—and free speech—can be detrimental to society.

My personal view is to support free speech and free press. But Wiesel makes a good point in light of the current state of affairs in our world, which is full of fake news, innuendos, and social media propaganda often created to stir hate and to feed negative personal agendas. In the highly competitive media space, networks race to be the first to provide "breaking news," often with content that has not been fully vetted to be factual and truthful. There needs to be strict regulation or some watchdog agency that makes certain that the public is provided with content that is factual, right, and truthful. Sure, this will create a bureaucracy—again not something I favor—but not addressing it is also a bad idea, as it will continue to divide our communities and potentially lead to dire circumstances. While I don't have the full solution, I do believe this dialogue is important.

Before Wiesel decided to pursue journalism, he had taken a job as a translator and editor for the weekly newspaper published in Paris by the Irgun pre-state underground organization, part of the Zionist movement. Wiesel would go on to write about the Jewish conflicts in Israel as a correspondent for the daily *L'Arche*. He was assigned to write about the arrival and absorption of new immigrants who had survived the Holocaust in Europe, but the tales he heard were harsh. Jewish immigrants were welcomed with criticism and discontent in Israel, and those hoping to escape humiliation found they were considered little more than human wreckage by their new hosts.

Throughout his career as a journalist, Wiesel pondered how to explain the plight of the Holocaust to those who couldn't understand it. The Holocaust, then considered throughout Europe as a taboo topic, had been suppressed to the point of almost being forgotten, yet the pain of the survivors and the anti-Semitism they faced were still very prevalent. So instead of staying silent—which Wiesel believed was part of the problem— he wrote of his experience, unearthing a piece of history that had yet to be properly dealt with.

Wiesel not only became a voice for Holocaust survivors and those experiencing anti-Semitism, but a voice for those who were facing injustice throughout the world. As a journalist, he has brought many cases to light; as a political activist, he has actively campaigned to correct them.

## Competency in Tackling Societal Issues

Elie Wiesel had forever changed the course of history with the publication of his memoir *Night*, which detailed his tragic experience as a young boy confined to the death camps of Nazi Germany. But his account proved to be so much more than a tale of death and despair; he forced a tragedy to the forefront of public consciousness with the hope that these evils might never be allowed to happen again.

Wiesel made "Holocaust" the term it is today, associating it directly with the extermination of over six million Jews during World War II by Nazi Germany. His unearthing of this harrowing event led many world leaders to erect memorials in remembrance to those who had been murdered, as well as openly discuss the Holocaust in schools. Survivors suddenly emerged from the shadows to share their own accounts, and many other books detailing the tragedy of the Holocaust were published after *Night*. The Holocaust Memorial Museum in Washington, DC, honors those who shared their stories and those who never had the chance to—its existence ensures this tragic piece of history will never be forgotten and will never be allowed to happen again.

Wiesel's memoir and work as an educator was influential in building the collective post-war memory of the Holocaust—a memory Wiesel infused with lessons on the dangers of indifference. He believed the greatest memorial possible for the victims would be to save future lives in memory of them. During the Holocaust, the world for the most part silently abandoned the Jews of Europe. This indifference allowed evil men to take power without resistance. Wiesel dedicated his work to ensure no other group would face a similar horror.

Wiesel's foundation has bettered the lives of thousands of refugee families and children escaping crisis in their homeland, as well as educated future leaders on the importance of acceptance, understanding, and intolerance. His legacy to society is reflected in the hope that one day we can look past our indifference and take a proactive approach against the injustice that is still so prevalent in our world.

## Competency in Spirit

Faced with possibly the worst things a human being could encounter, Wiesel admits to questioning his faith while imprisoned in the death camps. The Jewish people had been persecuted throughout history, but in Wiesel's most dire moments it seemed God and mankind had turned a blind eye. This is not to say Wiesel had abandoned his faith—if anything, his anger and protest only made it that much stronger.

While confined to the Buchenwald labor camp, Wiesel experienced the utter desperation of men fighting to survive. Sons turned on their fathers for extra scraps of food and often abandoned them in their own struggle to live. In his memoir Wiesel recalls an instance during his transportation to Buchenwald when a passerby had thrown bread into his wagon. With animal ferocity, starving men began to attack one another for bits of crust. When one old man emerged from the mob with a piece of bread hidden in his shirt, his son beat him to death for it. He didn't get far in devouring it, however—desperate men attacked the son, and two men died for that precious bread crust.

At the age of sixteen Wiesel resolved never to lose his humanity, no matter how hopeless the situation seemed. Any extra rations he managed to receive were given to his ailing father, even when it was apparent that he was dying. The Nazis and their death camps could not break his morale, and perhaps choosing to survive for the sake of another is what saved him.

Once liberated from the camp, Wiesel's determination to save others was reflected not only in his work as a journalist and political activist, but in his faith and spirit. He said in his Nobel lecture, "Mankind must remember that peace is not God's gift to his creatures, it is our gift to each other." In other words, man cannot rely solely on God to keep evil from occurring—the eradication of evil also relies heavily on man's righteous efforts.

Wiesel has said that the Holocaust occurred not because of the influence of one evil man, but because of the indifference of thousands. Had the Jews been given a voice outside their situation, perhaps help could have come sooner. Wiesel's life work focuses on battling this indifference, challenging world leaders and future influencers to take a proactive stance against genocide, racial cleansing, and other injustices that are being allowed to happen throughout the world.

## Question to Ponder

When we see societal ills, it is our responsibility to be accountable and either create viable effective and affordable solutions to those ills or get involved with those who are actively pursuing these changes. The important question to ask is, "Where am I in the world of indifference? Who do I need to forgive and reach out to?" To do this, you might also need to ask yourself, "Where do I stand on the plight of the other person?"

When my son was tragically murdered, I wondered how his grandfather and guardian was dealing with the fact that his grandson had murdered an innocent unarmed person. I felt we were both suffering an incredibly difficult and unresolvable dilemma. I reached out to him in forgiveness, letting him know that we both have lost sons and now we must come together and make sure no other parents and grandparents need to suffer what we have experienced. That eradicated indifference, and after twenty-five years we are still together working in the Tariq Khamisa Foundation and have developed a strong bond of brotherhood.

# 6

## MUBARAK AWAD
## PROMOTING NONVIOLENCE
## AND PEACE IN PALESTINE

*"Every human being is responsible for his or her action
even in the most difficult of situations. We have choices to make—
the choice to resist, to run away, or to do nothing."*

—*Mubarak Awad*

Mubarak Awad—often referred to as the "Palestinian Gandhi"—was a victim of senseless violence when his father was killed during the 1948 Arab-Israeli War, leaving him and his mother refugees in the Old City of Jerusalem. But despite his hardships as a child, Awad opted to pursue peace in place of revenge. He left Jerusalem for America in the 1960s and founded the National Youth Advocate Program, as well as the Youth Advocate Program International, both responsible for finding placements for "at risk" youth and children victimized by conflict, exploitation, and state and personal violence. In 1983 he brought his work back to Jerusalem and established the Palestinian Centre for the Study of Nonviolence, an organization promoting peaceful resistance and nonviolence to solve the conflicts between Palestine and Israel.

The history of the Israeli–Palestinian conflict began with the establishment of the state of Israel in 1948. This conflict came from the intercommunal violence in Mandatory Palestine between Israelis and Arabs from 1920 and erupted into full-scale hostilities in the 1947–1948 civil war. The conflict continues to the present day on various levels.

*We were fortunate to have Mubarak Awad share his own life story. He hopes his own experiences and his message of peace will resonate with the leaders of tomorrow:*

It is unfortunate that within my Palestinian culture we do not always keep our stories, facts, and history in written form. We have now lost record of a significant amount of the unique qualities inherent within the Palestinian nonviolent struggle. I base my own Palestinian nonviolent struggle on two fundamental criteria:

1) Religion/Spirituality: That as a human being, I, like all others, am a child of God. So for any person to kill the spirit of God found in every person is not right, no matter the circumstance.

2) Psychology: Despite our physical weaknesses, each human being has a right to resist injustice, the right to resist occupation, and the right to be free.

I was born into a loving family in Jerusalem, Palestine, in 1943. Just outside the gates of the old city, my father was killed by a Jewish terrorist group called Zionist Haganah during the Arab-Jewish fighting in 1948. When Zionism was being formulated, the predominant language spoken in Palestine was Arabic, and the majority of its inhabitants were Muslim. There was also a sizeable Christian minority consisting of a number of traditional Christian communities, the majority of which were Greek Orthodox, and a small minority of Jews, although there were not Zionists. Under the Ottoman Empire the land of Palestine was part of a larger region that included present-day Jordan, Syria, and Lebanon (all of which together were called *Al-Sham*), with Damascus functioning as the administrative capital of the area.

Zionism is a religious and political effort that brought thousands of Jews from around the world back to their ancient homeland in the Middle East and reestablished Israel as the central location for Jewish identity. When UN decided to partition Palestine into a Jewish and an Arab state, the Zionists agreed, but the Arab leadership refused to support it. Civil conflict between the two groups ensued immediately.

My mother was a great inspiration to my six brothers and me. When my father was killed, my youngest brother, Diana, was forty days old and my oldest brother, Nickola, was eleven. Diana and Nickola, as well as Bishara, Elizabeth, Ellen, Alex, and I could not leave our mother's side, fearing she'd be the next victim of this war. My father's murder shattered my family's foundation, and to add to our misery we were forced to leave our home the next day to go inside the gates of the Old City, leaving everything we knew behind, or risk being shot.

I've always wondered how we were able to overcome this great loss and survive in the midst of such a senseless, violent war. I know we can source much of our strength from my mother's faith in God and peaceful spirit in the face of hardship, which brought calmness to us all. She never wavered from the morals held within her Greek Orthodox Catholic upbringing, and she did not harbor a spirit of revenge or resignation. Instead, she was determined to have us believe that the person who killed our father did not know that he left a widow and seven children to raise. She told us, "Please don't take revenge for your father, don't kill anyone, don't ever destroy a human life"—that demand has resonated with me throughout my entire life.

Mother had no choice but to place us in orphan schools once we were inside the gate, which was horrible for me. For five or six years I never had a full stomach or enough to eat. Out of respect for my mother, however, I persevered with my studies. Fortunately, she was able to keep Nicola and Diana with her while she volunteered at a local hospital, eventually continuing her career as a nurse.

I finished school in Palestine and was able to come to the United States for a college education. After I completed my bachelor's degree in social work and sociology from Bluffton University in Ohio, I was granted US citizenship and decided to pursue my education even further by obtaining a PhD in child psychology from Saint Louis University. For a time afterward I settled in Ohio and established a statewide program to find homes for wayward youths ensnared by the criminal justice system, which evolved into the National Youth Advocate Program in 1978. But my heart still belonged to Palestine, and as youth violence began to become a huge issue during the war, I resolved to return to help the Palestinian children struggling through the war as I had.

I returned to Palestine in 1983 as a psychologist who was interested in counseling Palestinians. This was to be my contribution to the Palestinian cause, to commit myself to two years of training, where I would promote the need for child and school counseling programs.

I also wanted to bring to the attention of Palestinians a clear picture of what happens to a community under foreign occupation and to relay an understanding of the concept of being colonized by a group that has appeared to suffer more than most throughout history. It was a way to make known to Palestinians that justice would not merely be handed to them, that despite their lack of power, they had the right to resist occupation and the right to be free like any other group in the world. I wanted Palestinians to grasp that changes must be made in order to avoid having to depend on the goodwill and charity of Arabs and Muslims, the UN, the United States, or Europe.

It is with this intention that I opened the Palestinian Counseling Center in 1983, which sought to train school counselors and crisis centers to work with children and youth who had been affected by the war. It was crucial the next generation learn to cope with every situation—even something as tragic as losing a loved one to murder or prison—without harming themselves, an issue that was quickly becoming an epidemic.

Palestinian youth had become the symbol of violent resistance, most notably demonstrated in the first intifada in 1987, which began as a sort of rock-throwing children's crusade. All sectors of Palestinian society took part in periodical civil uprisings, but 60 percent of the population that participated were under the age of fifteen.

What would provoke unarmed children to take to the streets in protest against such a powerful army? The answer is somberly simple: They had spent their entire lives under Israeli occupation, deprived of the inalienable right to freedom. Throughout their childhoods, these youths had been living in towns and villages whose streets were patrolled daily by the soldiers of a foreign Israeli army. Periodically their schools were arbitrarily closed. They had seen family and friends thrown into prison and tortured. Their homes were often destroyed in response to defiance of the Israeli authorities, or for no reason at all, and they could be severely punished merely for displaying the colors of the Palestinian flag in public places or for writing slogans on walls. In addition, many had grown up witnessing their parents being humiliated at checkpoints and in house-to-house searches. Palestinian youth took to the streets to fight for their people's freedom and for basic human rights. In "Let Us Rethink Our 'Special Relationship' with Israel," American professor Charles Black Jr. had the following to say about the role of the Palestinian youth during the first intifada:

"They count themselves part of a people; they believe this people to be grievously wronged. Their oppressors, as they see the matter, need fear nothing, being armed and protected beyond the possibility of fear by a great power across the ocean—whose hostility to themselves they cannot understand. . . . They can expect nothing but cruelty. So, what do they do, these young Palestinians? Against huge odds, quite without real weapons or any other resources, they at last decline to submit, and instead go out on the streets and pick up stones."

What name shall we give to the trait of character that produces conduct like that? The word is *courage*. But at what point does courage come at much too high a cost? The next generation was partaking in violence and dying in hopes of stopping violence and death. I believed their courage must be channeled toward a different path.

After several years I came to an awakening that Palestinians need a shift in their ideas of resistance to end the Israelis' military occupation. I was confident that my fellow psychologists could continue the counseling work, so I chose to go in a different direction. I opened another center in Jerusalem the same year, the Palestinian Centre for the Study of Nonviolence, to bring actual facts, concerns, and alternative solutions to the Palestinians. My inspiration for the center drew from examples of nonviolence in the Islamic and Arabic cultures and from lessons learned by

Gandhi's satyagraha model in India and Martin Luther King Jr.'s peaceful demonstrations in the United States. The Palestinian idea of nonviolence, which I prefer to call steadfastness, or *sabar*, (meaning both "patient" and "cactus" in Arabic), reflects the Palestinian ingrained belief that through patient endurance we will ultimately triumph over occupation and aggression, as is reflected time and again throughout our history. This embedded cultural outlook saw the Palestinians through scores of invaders who occupied Palestine, only to give up over time and eventually withdraw. Thus, even during the worst days of violence in the Arab-Israeli conflict, the majority of Palestinians, until today, have steered clear of violence.

I found it important to help my compatriots understand that unlike all previous occupiers of our homeland, Israelis were a different kind of adversary. Many Jews around the world have been at the forefront of civil, human, student, and women's rights movements. In using our nonviolent approach in opposition to this particular opponent, I felt we ought to speak their language. It was an opportunity to use voices and moral concepts rather than bullets.

But in the midst of war, morality is often second tier. The first intifada, which began in 1987 and lasted till 1993, was a violent uprising that brought worldwide recognition to the Palestinian cause at a heavy price. In reaction to the uprising, three times more soldiers were deployed to the West Bank than the number used to conquer it during the Six-Day War in 1967. By the end of 1993, over one thousand Palestinians had been killed and many thousands more injured. Over sixteen thousand Palestinians were jailed, whizle on an average day twenty-five thousand Palestinians were under curfew. Property also took a heavy toll, with almost 2,500 houses demolished or sealed. During the same period, 481 Palestinians were deported.

Amnesty International and many others criticized Israel for using brutal methods to suppress the uprising. In 1988, after one such attack left its victims with serious injuries, UNRWA official Angela Williams told the *New York Times*, "We are deeply shocked by the evidence of the brutality with which people are evidently being beaten. We are especially shocked by the beatings of old men and women."

Despite the violence, during the first intifada some of the staunchest supporters of our cause were in fact Israelis and non-Israeli Jews committed to a nonviolent resolution. Unfortunately, as the second intifada (2000–2005) became even more bloody than the last as many of its nonviolent deposits were lost, most of these Jewish supporters lost faith in our movement.

During the first several years of the center's existence we initiated educational programs as well as the organization of small campaigns designed to involve more people in the nonviolent movement on a daily basis. An example of this was our protest against the eating and drinking of anything other than local products. Both the Israeli government and the Palestinian Liberation Organization rejected this method of nonviolent action, each for different reasons. The Israelis felt threatened by the Palestinian movement and took it seriously enough to bring in experts from around the world to determine a course of action should it take hold. On the other hand, the PLO took this movement as a challenge to their authority. They had not been consulted about ways in which resistance could take place without an arms race. Despite the opposition, the campaigns proved successful as they increased the use of the term "nonviolence." The concept began to seem less imported and Western.

Over time, we became more successful in relaying our message to rural villages, camps, and universities, while the urban cities remained skeptical. Our intent was to mobilize the Palestinian population and to confront occupation as a duty and responsibility, which belonged to every Palestinian, not just the political factions or the PLO. In doing this, we needed to extract the fear factor from both sides and show Palestinians that the Israeli soldiers were indeed human and could also feel pain and be influenced by a conscience. We visited villages and refugee camps on a regular basis and spoke to whoever would listen to our cause. It was our goal to assess the needs of the Palestinian people and to help them achieve their needs through practical methods of nonviolent resistance. This included acts like the planting of trees in order to deter the confiscation of land and cutting off water to the Israeli settlements whose pipes ran through Arab villages. Most notably, we requested that those who had lost or fled from their homes return and place a single rose where they used to live. Those who passed by and saw the roses were given a picture into the lives and spirits of the refugees. But perhaps the most important nonviolent resistance to Israeli occupation was the establishment of a functioning Palestinian society, which involved creating an infrastructure *independent* of Israel, through institutions such as schools, hospitals, factories, and other services.

Eventually, it was the small-scale spread of nonviolent activities in both Palestine and Israel that became a threat to the Israelis. It was a deliberate strategy involving Israeli peace groups in our campaign so that we could split the mind-set of the Israeli government. It gave us a chance to have partners on both sides working for the same goal of redeeming Palestinian aspirations without threatening the security of Israelis. Due to the success of the campaign, the Israelis felt it would be in their own interest to put a stop to my actions by imprisoning, and later, deporting me. In 1988 the Israeli government ordered me to leave Jerusalem, my home.

In the meantime, we assiduously sent students to different universities to study firsthand the ways of peace, conflict resolution, and nonviolence theories. The study of these practices positively led to the creation of more than thirty nongovernment organizations committed to our movement. They have since continued to apply these ideals in a more determined way in order to meet all of the challenges of both the Israeli occupation and higher ups in the PLO who opposed the nonviolent movement.

When traveling back to Palestine, even despite the poor economy, lack of freedom of movement, and deprivation of human rights by Israelis, I still find a favorable commitment to the nonviolent struggle today. I see that there is more of an acceptance for those who have tried to find their own sense of self by questioning authority and for those who desire inclusion in the political process. And most of all, I find myself steadfast in my patience for a positive outcome.

I continue to advocate for children, youth, and their families through the Youth Advocate Program International, an organization I established upon returning to the United States in 1996. YAPI provides alternative foster care and counseling to "at risk" youth and their families, offering our services to thousands of children, youth, and their families around the world each day. Our mission is to promote and protect the rights and well-being of the world's youth, giving particular attention to children victimized by conflict, exploitation, and state and personal violence. Throughout our existence we have brought aid to children and families who have suffered through modern child slavery, the HIV/AIDS crisis, commercial sexual exploitation, the exploitation of child soldiers, and discrimination against female children. YAPI strives to nurture the positive potential of young people, enabling them to become their own best advocates. Recently we have been working on programs to help our children and youth stop fundamentalism and bullying, understand equality, and bring those from every background together with the promise of a peaceful tomorrow.

I am also still very dedicated to the nonviolence movement I began in Palestine. Today I am president of Nonviolence International, which researches and promotes nonviolent action, a culture of peace, and seeks to reduce violence and passivity worldwide. We believe that all people of every culture and religion can employ appropriate nonviolent methods for personal fulfillment, positive social change and international peace. The main focus of the organization is promoting nonviolent solutions through the training and education of individuals, NGOs, and governments. The website is nvintl.net. nonviolentintrnational.org

Despite the ongoing violence in Israel, and the new wars that have claimed so many innocent lives around the world, I still have high hopes that the next generation will come to realize that violence will never lead to peace. With the invention and threat of chemical warfare, it is especially crucial today that people address rising tensions through strategic conflict resolution rather than an arms race. I wish that my example has inspired others to follow through with a dedication to nonviolent resistance, a dedication I believe can only lead to peace and understanding.

## Competency in His Field of Endeavor

Awad's career as a child psychologist had prepared him to make a difference in the lives of children worldwide. Although he drew from his own experiences as a child of war, his decision to further his education was crucial to understanding how and why at-risk youth are often drawn to lives of violence, allowing him to construct many successful programs targeted at alleviating the pain and suffering of children of all societies.

Awad has dedicated many years to training counselors within his organizations and similar organizations how to work with children who have been raised in seemingly hopeless situations, as he had. Having received an education in a refugee orphan school and going on to acquire a master's degree from a prestigious American university, Awad emphasizes the importance of education within his programs and works to send many at-risk youth to colleges and universities. He believes ignorance is often the cause of violence and emphasizes the importance of learning and understanding different histories and cultures found throughout the world.

The Palestinian Counseling Center, National Youth Advocate Program, Youth Advocate Program International, and Nonviolence International have all gained international attention and respect. Many world governments have reached out to Awad for training on how to eliminate youth violence in their countries, as well as how to integrate children who have been scarred from tragedy back into their communities. Awad claims he has never turned away a child or family in need of aid, and he will always continue to strive for a better world for the next generation.

## Competency in Tackling Societal Issues
Awad has dedicated his life to finding a resolution for one of the most violent conflicts of our lifetime. Many have hailed his movement as courageous—but too late. But Awad is determined that nonviolence and civil disobedience are, and forever will be, the only answer. Even today, though violence in Palestine has escalated to an all-time high, Awad has faith that the youth and the young people—people he had mentored through his own programs on both sides of the conflict—will recognize the senselessness of the violence taking place in their homes, on their streets, to their families, and to themselves.

In the meantime, Awad continues to preach nonviolence in conflicts happening around the world, including the Libyan and Syrian conflicts, the Syrian Civil War, and the Boko Haram insurgency in Africa. Until nonviolence is adopted, however, he continues to mend the wounds of the youth who have suffered at the hands of violence, hoping they will discover a peaceful resolution in their lifetimes that would make his organizations obsolete.

## Spiritual Competency
Although Awad had experienced one of the worst tragedies a child may endure—the murder of his father, seen before his own eyes—Awad never

faltered from the morals his mother relentlessly sought to make him understand.

As a young boy he realized that even the most evil people have a conscience—it is often morality that is lost in times of war. Awad remembered this as he counseled children and rallied his nonviolence supporters. When we are afraid, angry, threatened, or lied to, our morals become muddled as we make excuses for actions we otherwise would never condone. But our conscience—our spirit—knows better. How could a person reason with himself after killing peaceful protestors, women, and children? How could they kill a family when they have a family themselves? Awad's nonviolence movement sought to awaken the spirit of the people who sought violence as the answer, hoping they would realize that no sound human conscience could rationalize the killing of innocent civilians.

Of course, this movement has not been successful in ending the war—it is difficult to gain supporters when their minds are shrouded by as much revenge and hate as the perceived aggressors. Many will not take the time to connect with their spirits to discover the true outcome of their actions. Violence will not lead to peace, nor will it lead to resolution. Many more people will die, many more families will be destroyed, and many more children will lose hope until we begin thinking with our head, heart, and spirit as one.

## Question to Ponder

I am moved by Awad's commitment and courage. He does not hesitate and risks all in what he believes—a rare attribute to find in people. The important takeaway from this man is the concept of CANEI—Constant and Never-Ending Improvement—what that means is that tomorrow I will be a better person than I am today and even a better person the day after tomorrow than tomorrow. In other words, becoming a better person is a lifelong pursuit, and some sages posit that this continues into our next life and beyond. Both Mubarak and I live in this philosophy and understand that it is in the eventual perfection of our souls that we are eventually united with the one Source from whence we all came.

The question to ponder is, "Am I committed to the same philosophy of constant and never-ending improvement (CANEI)?" The important lesson here is one of service. We do not just live in our homes and work; we also thrive in our community. How much are you volunteering in service in your community? I spend twenty-five hours a week at Tariq Khamisa Foundation as a volunteer and have a strong sense of serving my community and beyond. While twenty-five hours is a lot—I am not complaining, as the work is very fulfilling—it is important that each one of us contribute to our communities through giving somewhere between 10 percent and 20 percent of our time to service. Another question to ponder is, "Where do I stand in community service?" It is important to share your time, treasure, and talent with your community. It is where happiness and joy live.

# 7

## DAISAKU IKEDA

## A CHAMPION OF PRACTICAL

## APPLICATION OF BUDDHIST HUMANISM

"A great inner revolution in just a single individual will help achieve
a change in the destiny of a nation and, further, will enable
a change in the destiny of all humankind."

—Daisaku Ikeda

Daisaku Ikeda, founder of Soka Gakkai International, one of the world's largest Buddhist lay organizations, was born in Tokyo, Japan, in 1928. Having survived the devastation of World War II as a teenager, Ikeda joined a youth group of the Soka Gakkai Buddhist Association in hopes of solving the fundamental causes of human conflict. This would become his lifelong work, eventually forming the global SGI movement and founding numerous institutions dedicated to fostering peace, culture, and education. He describes his vision for his organization as a "borderless Buddhist humanism that emphasizes free thinking and personal development based on respect for all life."

From humble beginnings as the son of seaweed farmers, Daisaku Ikeda offers a gleaming example of transformation from modest origins to achieving global impact. Ikeda's childhood years were met with various health struggles that included tuberculosis—an airborne disease that was notoriously deadly in densely populated Japan. It was due to these struggles that his doctors predicted he would not live past thirty. Little did his doctors know that prediction would spark within Ikeda a sense of motivation and purpose that served to his benefit throughout his long life.

Born as the fifth of eight children in 1928, Ikeda was notably marred by the devastation of World War II. Like many other young men at the time, Ikeda's four older brothers were drafted into military service. Though Ikeda himself was not drafted, the devastating effects of the war hit all too close to home. One day, he watched as his mother was handed a small white box that contained his eldest brother Kiichi's cremated remains, for he had been killed in battle. From the traumatic loss of his eldest brother dawned a newfound disgust for war, as well as a passion to work toward eradicating the root causes of human conflict.

Following the conclusion of the war, a period of disarray and confusion ensued in Japan. Cities were reduced to rubble, families and communities were shattered by the losses of loved ones, and society as a whole was struggling to regain its footing. Seeking to make sense of the postwar world, Ikeda turned to books on literature and philosophy for answers. In his quest for knowledge, at the age of nineteen he attended a meeting of the Soka Gakkai, a Buddhist lay movement that emphasized messages of self-empowerment and the promotion of peace. It was at this meeting that he met Josei Toda, a man who would later turn out to be the single most influential figure in Ikeda's life. You see, not long prior, the Soka Gakkai had been almost fully dismantled by the Japanese government, which had not taken kindly to the group's opposition to militaristic policies. In fact, Josei Toda was imprisoned for two years because of his objections. It was his enduring commitment to improving Japanese society—in spite of the abuse and persecution he had faced—that so greatly impressed Ikeda and drew the nineteen-year-old to follow him. The two men shared a vision of transformation for Japanese society and a belief in the deep potential of the individual person to effect peace. By virtue of Toda's mentorship, the direction of Ikeda's life was profoundly and forever altered.

Ikeda began working for Toda's publishing company in 1948, where he honed his literary skills as the editor of a magazine. At the same time, he attended night classes at a local college to continue to foster a well-rounded knowledge base. When financial hardships pushed Toda to the brink of collapse, he was forced to step away from his publishing business for the sake of protecting the Soka Gakkai organization. In this time of distress, Ikeda rose to the occasion and not only assumed the role of dealing with the publishing business's creditors, but also eventually helped Toda repay his debts. Remarkably, Ikeda sacrificed his salary, his quality of life, and even his health for the sake of supporting the mentor for whom he so deeply cared and admired. During this period of intense financial struggle, Toda crafted his vision for establishing schools and universities that operated under the *soka*, or value-creation, education philosophy. What may have seemed like an unattainable goal to some was a serious, achievable result in Ikeda's eyes.

Due to the sacrifices he made to support his mentor, Ikeda was forced to step away from his formal night schooling. In return, Toda pledged to personally provide Ikeda with a university-level education, based on his own vast personal knowledge and multidisciplinary prowess. But the education he sought to provide Ikeda wasn't limited to the metaphorical classroom. Rather, he shortly began placing his disciple in roles of greater and greater responsibility within the Soka Gakkai in hopes of honing his leadership skills too. Soon enough, Ikeda was appointed to a leading role within Tokyo's Kamata Chapter, where he quickly achieved remarkable success in expanding the chapter's membership.

Just a few years after the organization's vast expansion, in 1955, the Soka Gakkai made a push into political life—a decision that was founded in the belief that the political process and positive societal transformation were simply two sides of the same coin. As such, the organization fielded more than fifty of its members to run as independent candidates for local office. One year later, the group put six candidates forward in a national election for Japan's House of Councillors, and three of those candidates were elected. The unlikely triumph of these winning campaigns was spearheaded by none other than Daisaku Ikeda.

It became clear from this election that the Soka Gakkai was a national force to be reckoned with, boasting an extensive grid of grassroots support across the land. To Ikeda and the Soka Gakkai, this election was affirmation that their movement had teeth—that the Japanese people favored their message of individual empowerment and a transformation toward a more peaceful society. But to the established conservative and labor parties, this intrusion posed an imminent threat to their entrenched power. As a result, the established groups launched intimidation and media campaigns against Soka Gakkai members and their families, even going door-to-door to strong-arm members into denouncing the organization and their faith.

In spite of this persecution, the efforts of the Soka Gakkai persisted, with Ikeda steadfast in his commitment to the cause. Following the death of his beloved mentor in 1958, Ikeda eventually became the organization's third president and shepherded in a new era for the movement. Early in his tenure, Ikeda made the decision to establish the Komei ("clean government") political party, founded on the Buddhist principles of pacifism and humanism. By entering the political realm, Ikeda sought for the Soka Gakkai to be in a position to focus more wholly on the welfare of the Japanese people.

Over the course of the following decades, thanks to Ikeda's vision, the Soka Gakkai expanded abroad and Soka Gakkai International was born. Over time, Ikeda undertook a series of nonconventional diplomatic endeavors aimed at promoting dialogue, building cultural and social relationships, and sharing the message of the Soka Gakkai organization with the world. Both in his official presidential capacity and later on, Ikeda was committed to encouraging mutual understanding between leaders of various nations and cultures. In keeping with his Buddhist philosophy, Ikeda called upon the United Nations to marshal continued peace and prosperity for the nations of the world.

Today, Daisaku Ikeda remains a strong advocate for the values that drove him to become involved with the Soka Gakkai early in life. The promotion of peace, the innate sanctity of human life, and the betterment of society remain central tenets of his advocacy. To this day, he continues to write articles, essays, and books on the Buddhist philosophy in addition to supporting the mission of Soka Gakkai International across the globe.

## Competency in His Field of Endeavor

No matter the context, effective leadership requires an aptitude for clear communication and a passion for the issues at hand, and Ikeda's case is no different. His capacity for leadership was quickly made apparent through his successes with Tokyo's Kamata Chapter of the Soka Gakkai. As an organizer and local community leader, Ikeda helped the organization reach its national goal of seven hundred fifty thousand member households set by then-president Josei Toda. This degree of growth was unprecedented, yet Ikeda's tenacity and dedication to promoting peace helped facilitate the group's meteoric rise within Japan. Later, as president of the organization, his efforts brought about the global expansion of the group and the founding of Soka Gakkai International. Rather than looking inward and focusing exclusively within the borders of Japan, Ikeda recognized an opportunity to share the group's message of peace, understanding, and respect for the dignity and sanctity of human life with the world.

Initially, the organization's international presence was limited to war brides who had emigrated to the United States with their American husbands. Despite this fact, Ikeda recognized that an opportunity existed for the expansion of the Buddhist philosophy in nations other than Japan itself. As a result, he traveled around the world with the mission of expanding the Soka Gakkai's movement and facilitating greater engagement between his ideological compatriots and those individuals in positions to affect the positive outcomes he sought.

The expansion of Soka Gakkai International was not instantaneous, but rather it occurred over many years thanks to the tenacity of Ikeda and the members he inspired. Currently, it is estimated that there are nearly twelve million members of Soka Gakkai International across the globe. In addition, there are now more than a dozen Soka schools and universities worldwide, including the Soka University of America in Southern California.

## Competency in Tackling Societal Issues

The first half of the twentieth century in Japan witnessed a number of momentous shifts in both its domestic and international landscapes. The end of the imperial era and the devastation of World War II are just two of the factors that brought a great deal of turmoil and uncertainty to the nation.

Following the war, countless families and communities were irreparably damaged. Existing within many Japanese people at the time was a deep desire for societal change, moving away from the policies of militarism and toward a more peaceful and equitable society. But under the oppressive thumb of the wartime government, no avenue existed through which the Japanese people could truly materialize these beliefs. Thanks to the dedication of individuals like Josei Toda and Daisaku Ikeda, such an avenue came to prominence in the form of the Soka Gakkai.

The Soka Gakkai's membership did not explode by chance. It was because the organization's message resonated with everyday citizens who felt uncertain as to the futures of their families, their communities, and their nation. The Soka Gakkai spoke to peoples' weariness of conflict and desire for a more just, peaceful society. Ikeda's decision to formally enter Japanese politics was not a whimsical one. It was a strategic choice that resulted from an eagerness to enact structural change to Japanese government.

## Competency in Spirit

By all accounts, Ikeda was a visionary leader for the Soka Gakkai. Through shrouds of uncertainty and skepticism held by senior leaders of the organization, Ikeda ventured out on a path of immense magnitude and succeeded in garnering support across the globe. Such an endeavor required not only courage, but a genuine belief in the righteousness of his cause. As someone who had experienced the devastation of war and violent conflict at a young age, he made a decision to dedicate his life toward the betterment of civil society. This was no fleeting ambition, but rather a lifelong quest that spanned across numerous threats of large-scale conflict, including the Cold

War. In *The New Human Revolution*, vol. 11, Ikeda wrote about the threat posed by nuclear conflict and the convictions of his late mentor:

"President Toda also believed that, amid the Cold War's intensifying threat of nuclear weapons, it was the responsibility of Japan, as the only nation that had been the victim of a nuclear attack, to speak out against that threat and become a messenger of world peace. In order for Japan to rise to that role, he strongly felt that political leaders with a global consciousness—an awareness that we are all members of the same global community, which he called 'global citizenship'—were indispensable."

Today, the global presence of Soka Gakkai International is a testament to Ikeda's fortitude as a satyagrahi leader. His ability to turn tragedy into triumph offers us a gleaming example of pursuing constant and never-ending improvement for one's self and one's society, even in the face of adversity. From humble beginnings to global acclaim, Ikeda's dedication to improving society embodies the values of truth, peacemaking, and justice.

## Question to Ponder:

What stands out so strongly about Ikeda's life is his persistence. The untimely death of a close family member is a tragedy that few people experience, and yet Ikeda's loss sparked within him a desire to effect positive change in the world around him, so that others might be spared from the loss that had affected him so greatly. Where many people may have been defeated, he rose to meet the challenges that were presented to him, time and time again. While hard work and luck do not always win, persistence does. So the question for you to ponder is, "Where do you rate yourself in terms of your persistence?"

# 8

## WILMA MANKILLER

## REBUILDING A BROKEN NATION

*photo credit: The Wilma Mankiller Foundation*

*"The happiest people I've ever met, regardless of their profession,*
*their social standing, or their economic status,*
*are people that are fully engaged in the world around them."*

*—Wilma Mankiller*

One hundred fifty years after her great-grandfather and more than sixteen thousand Native Americans were forced Westward from their homes along the "Trail of Tears," Wilma Mankiller made it her purpose to revitalize the broken Cherokee Nation. She became the first elected female Principal Chief of America's second largest tribe in 1985, a position that had before then been male dominated and very conservative. Though her election was met with controversy and disapproval, Mankiller would soon become one of the nation's most popular and well-loved leaders. During her time in office she focused on improving the Cherokee Nation's government, health care, and education systems, as well as promoting community development in the most rural areas. Her reign saw the population of Cherokee citizens more than triple from fifty-five thousand to one hundred ninety-six thousand due largely to her founding of the community development department. Even after personal battles with numerous injuries and illnesses led her to turn down reelection, Mankiller continued to be an activist for Native Americans as well as women's rights, earning her induction to the Women's Hall of Fame in 1993 and the Medal of Freedom in 1998, America's highest civilian honor.

Wilma Mankiller was the sixth of eleven children born into a poor family in Tahlequah, Oklahoma, in 1945. She was raised on a one hundred sixty-acre tract known as "Mankiller Flats," given to her great-grandfather as part of a settlement the federal government made for forcing Native Americans from their tribal lands in the Carolinas and Georgia in the 1830s. Her home had no electricity, plumbing, or telephones, but Mankiller never recalled feeling poor on her family's plot in Oklahoma. Though her family lacked basic amenities, they were surrounded by a tight-knit Native American community all of the same class. But Mankiller's father, Charlie Mankiller, believed he could make a better life for his family in California and accepted a government offer for them to relocate as part of a relocation policy of the Bureau of Indian Affairs, whose goal was move Indians off federally subsidized reservations with the promise of jobs in America's biggest cities.

Once the family arrived in San Francisco in 1956, however, promises made by the federal government were not kept, money and aid did not arrive, and employment was often scarce. Mankiller also began to feel incredibly homesick. In *Mankiller: A Chief and Her People,* she described the move as her own "Trail of Tears":

"The United States government, through the Bureau of Indian Affairs, was again trying to settle the 'Indian problem' by removal. I learned through this ordeal about the fear and anguish that occur when you give up your home, your community, and everything you have ever known to move far away to a strange place. I cried for days, not unlike the children who had stumbled down the Trail of Tears so many years before. I wept tears . . . tears from my history, from my tribe's past. They were Cherokee tears."

After graduating high school, Mankiller met and married Hector Hugo Olaya de Bardi in 1963, and soon after they had two daughters together. She settled into her domestic role as wife and mother, but the political and social unrest that characterized the 1960s would have a life-altering effect on Mankiller, namely the occupation of an abandoned prison by Native American college students.

In 1969, San Francisco State student Mohawk tribe member Richard Oakes, along with other Native Americans of varying tribes, took charge of the abandoned prison on Alcatraz Island to call attention to the mistreatment and exploitation of Native Americans by the US government. She felt the students' demonstration articulated her own feelings about being a Native American, and she began a commitment to serve the Native American people to the best of her ability in the area of law and legal defense. This demonstration led to Mankiller's political awakening.

With her new promise to herself and her community, Mankiller began taking courses at a community college and later at San Francisco State

University. Her newfound confidence and independence created a strain in her marriage as she became more active outside the confines of her family. In 1974 she and Hugo divorced, leaving her a single head of household. She was left with her two young daughters, Felicia and Gina, and vowed to raise them as strong, independent, and proud Cherokee women.

In 1976 Mankiller returned to Oklahoma with her two daughters, found a job as a community coordinator in the Cherokee tribal headquarters, and enrolled in graduate courses at the University of Arkansas. Her classes and new career required her to drive long distances each day. One morning in 1979, Mankiller was returning home when a car approached her on a blind curve and another car attempted to pass it. Mankiller swerved to miss the approaching car but failed, colliding almost head-on. Mankiller was seriously injured, and many feared she wouldn't survive. Though her situation was grim, she was more fortunate than the other driver, who had died from the impact. That driver turned out to be her best friend, Sherry Morris. In addition to the major physical injuries Mankiller had to overcome, she also dealt with crippling guilt and loss after the accident.

The car accident was not Mankiller's only trial during this time. Soon after her move to Oklahoma it was discovered that she had inherited the kidney problems that had killed her father just a few years prior. Her early symptoms could be treated, though eventually she had to have a transplant. Her brother Donald became her "hero" after donating one of his kidneys so that she could live.

Then in 1980 Mankiller was diagnosed with myasthenia gravis, a muscle disease characterized by weakness and rapid fatigue of many of the muscles under voluntary control. Her life was threatened again, but her will to live and determination to follow through with her plans to help her people proved stronger.

Despite her challenges, Mankiller became an instrumental part of the Cherokee community while simultaneously completing her bachelor's degree in social sciences, taking graduate courses in community planning, and raising her daughters. She began volunteering in tribal affairs and leading campaigns for new health and school programs like Head Start, which provides comprehensive early childhood education to low-income children and their families. Her charisma did not go unnoticed—she was soon promoted to an economic stimulus coordinator for the Cherokee Nation, emphasizing community and self-help.

In 1981 Mankiller founded the community development department of the Cherokee Nation. She sought to improve Cherokee communities nationwide through the development and maintenance of new sanitation facilities, construction and maintenance of roads and public transit, and implementation of standard environmental health protocols, community youth development organizations, and community outreach programs. For the department's first major project, Mankiller helped develop a sixteen-mile waterline to Bell, Oklahoma, where many residents still had no indoor plumbing. The tribe provided equipment and technological assistance, while Bell residents—many of whom were Cherokee citizens—contributed most of the labor on a volunteer basis. The project's success led the tribe's principal chief, Ross Swimmer, to select Mankiller as his running mate in his reelection campaign in 1983.

Despite her many successful projects completed while a member of the Cherokee government, news of Mankiller's running for deputy chief was met with denunciation and judgment—not for her stand on any issue in particular, but because she was a woman running for a "man's role" within the tribe. She experienced rampant sexism and even death threats during and long after the election, but her experience proved her competent enough to accept the powerful role. Swimmer and Mankiller were elected into office, where Swimmer would serve for two years before being nominated to head of Bureau of Indian Affairs in 1985. Mankiller then replaced

Swimmer as principal chief of the Cherokee Nation, the first woman ever to be named chief of a major American Indian tribe.

Due to worsening health problems, Mankiller did not seek reelection in 1995. But she remained a driving force in tribal affairs and was often called to counsel and mediate among her successors. She was also appointed by then-President Bill Clinton as an adviser to the federal government on tribal affairs. She remained an activist for Native American rights, urging American Indians who had the right to vote to do so in order to elect officials who would address Native American issues in Congress. In addition, Mankiller fought for women's rights and the end to violence against women while giving lectures and heading protests at universities nationwide.

In 2009, she was awarded an honorary doctorate at Northeastern State University. In her commencement speech, Mankiller told attendees: "The happiest people I've ever met, regardless of their profession, their social standing, or their economic status, are people that are fully engaged in the world around them. The most fulfilled people are the ones who get up every morning and stand for something larger than themselves. They are the people who care about others, who will extend a helping hand to someone in need or will speak up about an injustice when they see it."

After nearly thirty years of activism, Mankiller died April 6, 2010, at her home near Tahlequah, Oklahoma, due to pancreatic cancer. She is remembered for the tenacity that she claims was due to her Cherokee blood, and for the same will that helped her overcome three potential life-ending events, to rebuild what is now one of the nation's strongest and most recognized Native American tribes.

## Competency in Her Field of Endeavor

Mankiller used her time in office to invoke radical change among the Cherokee Nation. She focused her attention on community development projects and organizations, establishing more tribally owned businesses, improving infrastructure, constructing new schools, job-training centers, and health clinics, and, perhaps most importantly, redefining the relationship between the tribe and the US government. She improved federal trade negotiations under the US federal policy of Native American determination, which refers to the social movements, legislation, and beliefs by which tribes within the United States exercise self-governance and decision-making on issues that affect their own people. Mankiller helped set a mutual understanding and respect between the Cherokee Nation and the United States that holds steady to this day.

Despite a call for modernization among Cherokee communities, Mankiller also stressed the importance of history and honor among her people. As the tribe's leader, she was the principal guardian of centuries of Cherokee tradition and custom. She would often refer to inspirational stories of strong-willed ancestors with a determination unique to the tribe, rallying the community—especially the youth—to revitalize their Cherokee pride and join in her cause. Mankiller's call to action reached voters as she was reelected principal chief in 1987 and again in 1991, this time with 83 percent of the votes. From 1987 to 1984, tribal revenue doubled to $150 million a year and enrollment nearly tripled from fifty-five thousand to one hundred ninety-six thousand.

## Competency in Tackling Societal Issues

As a community leader, Mankiller recognized the challenges among her people. It was apparent that many Cherokee reservations and communities were hindered by lower-than-national-average education levels, poor healthcare services, low employment, substandard housing, and deficient economic structure. By the time she took office in 1983, almost a quarter of Native American families were living below the poverty line.

Despite the criticism she received due to her being a woman in a powerful role, Mankiller was able to utilize her past challenges to her advantage.

By speaking of her own struggles with poverty, her humbling and enlightening experiences in San Francisco, and her prevailing spirit over her constant health battles, Mankiller sparked a new hope in her nation. Her unrelenting pride inspired many to trust in her and volunteer their services to revitalize their communities. As the first woman chief of the Cherokee Nation, she created a job center, increased the number of tribal health clinics, and brought jobs and businesses to the Cherokee jurisdiction. Summer programs for young people and increasing adult literacy were also a priority. Under Mankiller, poverty decreased by nearly 50 percent.

Mankiller was also an important role model for young Cherokee girls. Historically, women on reservations held the roles of wife and mother with little opportunity to excel in the workplace. In 1991 she worked with the American Association of University Women Tahlequah Branch and received a Community Action Grant to establish a mentoring program for girls at Sequoyah High School, a boarding school for Native American children. Girls were matched with career mentors, whom they shadowed throughout the program. Mankiller assisted in the process of locating Cherokee mentors for the girls. Designed to bolster self-confidence and opportunities for Native American girls, the program was a success.

## Competency in Spirit

Despite having grown up destitute and becoming content as a young wife and mother at seventeen, Mankiller felt a calling that struck deep beneath the surface. She abandoned her comfortable life to take on a role she knew would require incredible amounts of work and dedication toward a cause much bigger than herself. But instead of shying away from the challenge, Mankiller embraced the independence and purpose she found within herself through community involvement and volunteer work. On top of the responsibility of caring for her young daughters alone, Mankiller completed schoolwork and earned a respectable position within the Cherokee government. Her strong resolve and passion toward her work drove her to run for the highest elected position, and her early successes proved her worthy. Though the Cherokee people were skeptical of a woman chief, she soon became one of their most adored leaders.

Mankiller experienced her first call-to-action as a young mother, living a comfortable life with two young daughters and a husband. After her encounter with the student demonstrations in 1969, Mankiller could not ignore the fire that had sparked within her spirit. She recognized her duty to her community and, while many would have chosen to ignore the problems at hand, Mankiller stepped up.

It was this drive that led her to find her confidence and independence, though it drove her husband to divorce her. She spent her days supporting and caring for her daughters, going to class, and working, and her nights studying. Any free time she had was dedicated to the community, participating in protests and workshops for Native Americans. Even critical injuries and health scares could not slow down her progress—if anything, they made her even more determined.

Once elected Chief, her tenacity inspired an entire nation to rise up with her. She addressed issues that had long been ignored and, though she held on to the importance of traditional tribal customs, she helped shed light on outdated practices and old ways of thinking. She helped a broken nation regain its pride, and helped future generations find hope of becoming more than they dreamed they could ever be.

## Question to Ponder:

Mankiller was such a role model to many young Cherokee girls. I have always encouraged young people to find role models, especially in their own genders. It has helped me to continue to grow as a leader. This reminds me of a talk I recently gave at SDSU. At the end of my talk, a young man came up to me and said, "Mr. Khamisa, you changed my life." I asked him to share more, and here is what he said: "When I was in seventh grade, you came to speak at my school, and I chose you to be my role model and follow in your footsteps to be in financial services. I just graduated in finance and have a job at Wells Fargo bank. I did not follow my older brother, my father, and my grandfather, who were all gang involved." So the question for you to ponder is, "Where do you stand as a role model for the younger generation?"

# 9
## KAZUO INAMORI
## A DEVOUT SPIRITUAL ENTREPRENEUR
## AND GENEROUS PHILANTHROPIST

"People have no higher calling than to strive for
the greater good of humankind and society."
—Kazuo Inamori

Kazuo Inamori is a Japanese entrepreneur and founder of Kyocera and KDDI, CEO of Japan airlines, founder of the Inamori Foundation, creator of the Kyoto Prize, and a devout Zen Buddhist priest. Inamori has always paired his success as a businessman with philanthropic acts of generosity, hoping to inspire the next generation's leaders through ethical leadership and making significant contributions for the betterment of society. Throughout his career Inamori has made outstanding contributions to progress in science and chemistry, as well as to civilization and humankind through numerous scholarships and grants. Each year his foundation awards the Kyoto Prize to Japanese citizens who have made significant contributions to society, similar to the Nobel Prize in America.

In 1932 in Kagoshima, Japan, Kazuo Inamori was born to a father who made paper bags by hand for a living and a mother who aided her husband's work. As a child, Kazuo's uncle lived with his family under full-time care, as he was suffering from a debilitating case of tuberculosis. Despite his best efforts to avoid catching the disease, Inamori contracted the illness at just thirteen years old. Growing up during the Second World War, Inamori's family was forced to leave their home when it was destroyed by an air raid, so they sought greener pastures elsewhere in Japan. Fortunately, his tuberculosis disappeared upon the family's move, but he was still barred from attending public schools due to the fact that he had previously carried the illness. So he was forced to attend private schools. Because his family was poor, the prospect of attending high school seemed out of reach for quite a while. Finally, he was allowed to attend high school with his father's permission and the support of his former teachers. While in high school, he worked to support his family as much as he could, selling as many paper bags as he could physically bring along on his bicycle.

Despite dreams of becoming a medical doctor, he was met with heartbreak when he was unable to pass the entrance exams of his desired university. Instead, he attended Kagoshima University and graduated with a bachelor of science degree in applied chemistry in 1955. Shortly thereafter, he began a researcher role at Shofu Industries in Kyoto, where he quickly excelled and helped to develop an insulator for high frequency radio waves known as forsterite.

Just twenty-seven years old, in 1959 he left Shofu Industries to start Kyocera Corporation with the help of a three-million-yen investment from acquaintances and former colleagues. Kyocera began developing a variety of ceramic materials, such as electronic, engineering, and structural ceramics. Inamori's expertise was almost immediately recognized, and parts manufactured by Kyocera were used on spacecraft as part of the United States' Apollo Program that sent astronauts to the moon. Even the technology company International Business Machines (IBM) recognized Kyocera's specialized product offering, placing an order as large as twenty-five million parts at one point.

With the smashing success of Kyocera Corporation, Inamori moved into other industries as well. In 1984, Japan finally deregulated its telecommunications market, which had experienced nearly one hundred years of monopoly rule. Thanks to the industry's deregulation, Inamori decided to launch a telecommunications company, and his brainchild (today known as KDDI) has grown to become the second-largest provider in Japan.

Years later, in 2010, Japan Airlines (JAL) was in crisis—the company had entered into bankruptcy proceedings and was in dire need of new leadership. As a result, the Japanese government asked Inamori to step in as CEO to reconstruct the firm. He accepted and began the process of revitalizing the company by shifting employee attitudes toward work and customers, as well as implementing his personal management philosophy. Thanks to Inamori's leadership through its restructuring, Japan Airlines was finally allowed to re-list on the Tokyo Stock Exchange in 2012.

Outside of his business endeavors, Inamori is also a renowned philanthropist. Back in 1984 he established the Inamori Foundation, known for its awarding of the Kyoto Prize. Similar to the Nobel Prize, the Kyoto Prize is bestowed "as a means of recognizing persons who have made outstanding contributions to the progress of science, the advancement of civilization, and the enrichment and elevation of the human spirit." Awarded annually, the Kyoto Prize recognizes and encourages both scientific and spiritual achievement.

To date, Inamori holds numerous posts outside of the business world. These include serving as honorary chairman of the Kyoto Chamber of Commerce and Industry, foreign member of the Royal Swedish Academy of Engineering Sciences, trustee emeritus of the Carnegie Institution of Washington, and foreign associate of the National Academy of Engineering in the United States.

## Competency in His Field of Endeavor

Simply put, there is little debate as to the degree of success of an individual like Kazuo Inamori. In his chosen fields he has exhibited incredible business acumen over the course of his career, and it certainly shows. In 2018, Kyocera boasted a jaw-dropping $14.2 billion in sales, and the company sits at #90 on the Forbes List of Top Regarded Companies of 2018. Few individuals in the history of mankind have ever approached the level of success that he has achieved.

Even early in his career, Inamori was faced with challenges that required high levels of innovation, problem-solving, and attention to detail. For one of IBM's early orders from Kyocera, the American firm desired millions of highly specialized parts that required advanced skills to produce. Even though some doubted Inamori due to his relative youth in the industry, IBM believed in his capabilities. He struggled tirelessly for two years to develop a suitable product and to perfect the production process, and eventually he succeeded. The level of tenacity and work ethic exhibited in that instance undoubtedly contributed to the success of his career. Following IBM's twenty-five-million-part order, a slew of new orders began rushing in, causing the company to grow rapidly. By 1980 Kyocera had opened an office in California, and soon after the firm had expanded across the globe.

## Competency in Tackling Societal Issues

Prior to the deregulation of Japan's telecommunication's market, monopoly control over the industry led to incredibly high costs and incredibly low accessibility for the people of Japan. Even with equivalent technologies, it was nine times more expensive to use a phone in Japan than it was in the United States at the time. In the eyes of Kazuo Inamori, this was unacceptable—people needed to use phones every day, so why should a Japanese person have to pay so much more than others?

When the market was liberalized, Inamori's venture made waves in the industry. Very shortly, costs sank for the Japanese people and telephones became exponentially more accessible as a result.

In other areas of his business, too, Inamori sought to blend his business interests with broader societal interests. For example, Japan as a nation is not rich in natural energy resources, such as oil and natural gas. To address this concern, Inamori's company developed a more advanced and efficient photovoltaic battery to be used to store solar energy collected by private residences. This innovation served the dual purpose of reducing Japan's environmental footprint, while at the same time making electricity more affordable for the average Japanese citizen.

Moreover, nothing speaks more to Inamori's commitment to tackling societal issues than his establishment of the Inamori Foundation and the creation of the Kyoto Prize. At the time of its creation in 1984, the foundation was endowed with twenty billion yen in cash and Kyocera stock, ensuring its longevity for years to come. Inamori's remarks concerning the award underscore his dual reverence for both industrial and spiritual pursuits. In his philosophy statement for the Inamori Foundation, he says:

"Those worthy of the Kyoto Prize will be people who have, as have we at Kyocera, worked humbly and devotedly, sparing no effort to seek perfection in their chosen professions. They will be individuals who are sensitive to their own human fallibility and who thereby hold a deeply rooted reverence for excellence. Their achievements will have contributed substantially to the cultural, scientific, and spiritual betterment of mankind. Perhaps most importantly, they will be people who have sincerely aspired through the fruits of their labors to bring true happiness to humanity."

As evidenced by his words and actions, Inamori's example reminds us that the betterment of society is not only a noble pursuit but also a fruitful one.

## Competency in Spirit

As a devout, ordained Zen Buddhist priest, spirituality underpins much of Inamori's professional and philanthropic background. His life story presents a perfect counterexample to a claim that is made far too often in today's discourse: that rightfully guided spiritual values cannot go hand in hand with the pursuit of monetary wealth. From Inamori's example, it becomes clear that excellence in a professional field of endeavor can be achieved *without* sacrificing moral and spiritual guiding values.

The Zen Buddhist practice is noteworthy in that it presents no particular creed or doctrine, but rather emphasizes the individual practitioner's ability to connect with his or her innermost self. There are no commandments in the Zen practice, and no covenants the likes of the Judeo-Christian tradition. Instead, we observe the Zen practice manifest more subtly through Inamori's leadership. Unlike so many other businesspeople, and despite the various financial interests involved in any company's operations, Inamori remains devoted to ensuring the satisfaction of his employees. Through his outlook, material wealth is simply a byproduct of conducting business with a deeper spiritual purpose in mind.

## Question to Ponder

Inamori uses the perfect balance of business entrepreneurship, spiritual devotion, and philanthropic generosity to better society. He's an exemplary leader. The question for you to ask here is, "How do I balance and excel in my home life, work life, spirituality, and community service work?"

# IO
# REMY KHAMISA
# IN MEMORY OF MAMA

*"Mama always believed that everything happens for the good.
She reminded me many times that when one door closes, four new
ones open. She modeled an unwavering faith in the Universe."*
*—Azim Khamisa*

Mothers are the most important influential forces any human will encounter—we are born by them, raised and molded by their hands, and guided to become contributing members of our societies. Without mothers or mother figures, who would we have become?

My mother was a pursuer of peace, compassion, and servitude, a teacher of morality, and a leader to those who sought comfort in the most difficult of times. Her enormous heart and dedication to faith inspired everyone fortunate enough to meet her. I am forever grateful to her for instilling these qualities in me.

Remy Khamisa, my beloved mother, a strong-willed and determined woman, the matriarch to the Khamisa family, and an equally important member of her maiden Ahamed family, entered immortality surrounded by her loved ones on April 28, 2017, in Vancouver, Canada. The setting was a beautiful hospice reminiscent of a sacred temple, and my mother was enveloped by the abundant love emanating from her immediate family and the compassionate staff who cared for her till the end.

My mother turned eighty-seven on February 2, 2017; two months later, she suffered a massive stroke. She spent her last ten days on earth in Lions Gate Hospital and the North Shore Hospice. Her entire family, many well-wishers, friends, and community members were able to pay their final respects with nonstop prayers during her last few days. Though there were tears, those ten days were also filled with smiles, laughter, and hope.

Mama, as her family referred to her, spent her entire life in the service of her family, her community, and God. As a devout follower of the Ismaili faith, Mama prayed twice a day, every day, as expected of the Sufi tradition. For more than seventy years, she arrived at the Jamat Khana every morning at 3:00 a.m. to prepare tea, coffee, and cookies for the worshippers who came to meditate at 4:00 a.m., then returned again for nightly prayer. It was only when she fell ill during her last few months that she allowed herself to miss Jamat Khana, and she continued her spiritual practice at home despite being bedridden.

In many ways, her final gift was to bring the entire family and many others she had touched together for those last ten days. It was a loving reminder of the importance of the family customs and values she worked so hard to have us follow. She taught us that every member of the family has a duty and a responsibility to keep our family together and intact—she fulfilled her duty even through her passing.

My mother, Remy Ahmed, was born February 2, 1930, in Mumbai, India. My grandmother and her family lived in Mbale, Uganda, but my grandmother had traveled while very pregnant to India, where our ancestry is, and her daughter was born there.

From the moment she was born, my mother held a unique and special place in her family's hearts, especially her father's. While my grandmother, Sara, was pregnant with my mom, my grandfather, Gulamhussein, received the news that his sister, Sheru, was severely unhappy in her marriage in India. This warranted a trip to India by ship, which, though it was the fastest mode of transportation at the time, took weeks from Africa. When my grandfather and grandmother finally reached India, they found they were too late—Sheru had died. But the grief of death was soon replaced with the joy of new life, as my mother was born soon after. My grandfather declared his beloved sister had come back reincarnated as my mother, and from that day forward my mother and her father would always share an incredible bond.

My mother was the second born of six siblings—one older brother, three younger brothers, and a sister—and was raised in Uganda. Her father, my grandfather, worked in a cotton factory as a laborer to support his wife and seven children (one of whom died as an infant). Times were rough then—World War II was on the horizon and food in their village was rationed. My grandmother began catering to help my grandfather with the finances of their growing family. My grandparents lived in a two-bedroom house—all the children shared one room. My mother said they had to add a lot of water to the curry to feed the whole family.

Her family had to work very hard for very little, but Mama recalls her childhood as the best days of her life. Her home was always filled with friends, family, laughter, and so much love despite the constant hunger pangs they endured. My grandmother always greeted guests with open arms and was adamant the family share half the food on their own plates with them, a Muslim custom that was upheld despite having little food to offer. Her hospitality never faltered through harsh times.

Religion played an important role in Mama's life growing up and would continue to be a guiding force throughout her life. Her parents were devout Ismaili Muslims—they never cursed, smoked, or drank—and their daily routines followed Muslim values and customs. Her family woke up at four o'clock every morning to attend morning meditation at Jamat Khana, a daily practice that would become routine even as Mama started her own family and moved overseas. During school exams, 4:00 a.m. meditation was replaced with morning study groups as all the children would come together to prepare for tests. Mama was a very dedicated student and always at the top of her class. She hoped to become a nurse one day. But she never finished her schooling; during especially hard times, her father had no choice but to pull her out so she could help him earn money as a seamstress and help her mother as a caterer.

The dedication she demonstrated in her schoolwork she now placed on supporting her family. While her parents worked, she would watch her six siblings and keep house while helping make money in her spare time. With her father's help and motivation, Mama became an amazing seamstress at a very young age—the dazzling dresses she'd later create for her own daughter, granddaughters, and nieces were evidence of years of practice and perfection. She was also a very passionate chef and would relish the opportunity to have the lady with an English cookbook demonstrate to her how to make sweet cakes and cookies. She was especially diligent at perfecting her baking, and when she finally conquered a new recipe her father would boast to friends and family, "Come over, Remy has baked the most amazing English sweets!" Throughout her life, Mama would always show her love through the food she cooked.

Mama was forced to grow up quickly to support her family and her siblings, but when she became a teenager it was decided it was time for her to begin a family of her own. Her father began scoping for the best family with which to place his beloved daughter. His friend, Kassam Khamisa, was quick to suggest his nephew, Noordin Khamisa, as a possible candidate for marriage. My father agreed and arranged to meet Noordin for tea, to be served by my mother, the bride-to-be, a custom typical of Ismaili families. Mama was told to wear her best dress and a head scarf, but she was not aware she'd be serving tea to her potential husband till right before the party. Mama would have been only fifteen at the time, and she was so shy she couldn't even look at Noordin! Although it's unlikely my father would have noticed—he was so bombarded with questions from his future in-laws that he hardly had time for conversation, much less eye-contact, with his future bride. They asked all the important questions that would make any potential marriage candidate squirm in their seats: "Where do you work?", "How much money do you make?", "Do you pay Tithe?" Apparently, they felt confident in his response, and they decided to entrust Mama to him.

According to the Ismaili custom of the time stating that weddings would be arranged by family elders, Mama's father and her husband's uncle arranged for the two to marry in 1946. Thus, Mama was sent to begin her new life with a man she had yet to have a conversation with.

Before my father proposed to my mother in Kenya, he had a colossal falling out with his father. He moved out of his home and became estranged from his family. My parent's engagement was lengthy and not customary—Mama and my father were engaged by way of the heads of Jamat Khana, since his father would not get involved. Still, my father was determined to make it work. In times when jobs were precious, my father was incredibly fortunate to be offered a job at Motor Mart in Uganda through his close friend, Shermohamed. He used his first paycheck to rent a small, modest two-bedroom apartment in Kampala, and he, along with his grandmother, Awalbai, his stepbrother, and one of his closest friends, moved in together. The apartment was far from Motor Mart; my father bought a bicycle to get to and from work, though the trip back home was a grueling uphill climb. But despite his humble accommodations, my father's efforts paid off. With a steady career and a place to live, my parents were married on May 8, 1946, by our imam of the time, Sir Sultan Muhammad Shah.

It took my mother a long time to adjust to married life. She continued to take orders for dresses and cater with the help of Shermohamed's wife, but the work was not met with the same cheerful manner it had been before. Her new role as wife and matriarch of her family overwhelmed her with new responsibilities, and it was difficult to find joy or satisfaction in her prior work. She went from being a queen back home to being little more than a housekeeper in her married household.

A few months after moving in with her husband, Mama wrote to her father about her distress. She told him how Awalbai dictated what they would eat, how it was to be cooked, when they would eat, and just about everything else. She began to feel like a slave in her own home. Mama knew she couldn't express her frustrations to her husband, who had been raised by his grandmother and out of respect would never favor his wife, even if his grandmother was being unreasonable. She felt she hadn't received any support from her husband since the wedding. He was obsessed with moving up within the business and hardly ever had time for intimate conversations with Mama.

She was beginning to feel her faith falter, replaced with the tedious duties she was expected to fulfill from the moment she woke up to the minute she was allowed to fall asleep. Cooking, cleaning, sewing, abiding to Awalbai's every whim, repeat—this was her life now. Her religion was her map to navigating her difficult life—without Jamat Khana, community, and daily ritual, coping seemed useless. Mama was so conflicted and alone in her new marriage and wanted so desperately the relationships and support she had received from her family growing up. All she wanted was to come back home, even if it meant working as a seamstress for the rest of her life.

But her father's response to her anguish lacked sympathy. Though he missed her most of all after her marriage to my father, he responded that he had put his family's reputation in her hands when marrying her off, and that she must do what it takes to make the marriage work. His retort may have seemed harsh, but it was very typical of Muslim family customs in those days. Despite her grievances, he believed the marriage best for his daughter and his family.

On August 13, 1947, Mama gave birth to her first child—my sister Yasmin. Any mother would have been ecstatic with the arrival of their first baby and the beginning of their own family, but while Mama loved her daughter immensely, she dreaded the new responsibilities of motherhood.

When Mama was born, aunts, sisters, and grandmothers all came to help with the new baby. Cooking, cleaning, and caring for the baby became a family affair as the new mother watched and learned, giving her time to adjust to her new title. But Mama was not given the luxury of family support—her husband was estranged from his family, and her own family lived miles away. While my mother had grown up caring for her brothers and sisters, it did little to prepare her for the responsibility of her own baby. My mother did everything she thought a good mother should do—she checked on Yasmin when she cried late at night, she prepared the milk and the meals for the baby, changed diapers, rocked her to sleep. And she did all of this completely alone, save for Awalbai, who would often criticize her parenting methods and point out every mistake she made— "The baby has a rash; you left the dirty diaper on too long," or "That baby just cries and cries—it must be your baby food." She loved her Yasmin, but she was exhausted.

By October that same year, Mama's father took ill and passed away at the young age of forty. When my parents heard of his illness, they took the first bus from Kisumu to Kampala but arrived too late. Mama's father was gone, and with him that irreplaceable bond they had held since her birth. Her strongest supporter was gone, and Mama felt her hope start to slip away.

Mama gave birth to me on February 10, 1949. I was a happy, healthy baby, and my father was very excited to have a son. But with the jubilance of a new son came more sorrow for my mother and her family. When I started walking, it came as a shock that Yasmin, who was born almost a year and half prior, had yet to take her first steps. Mama took her to the doctor, but they could find nothing wrong with my sister and brushed off Mama's concern. But soon Yasmin began to cry and cry in the middle of the night, and my mother was at a loss trying to console her. She rushed Yasmin to the doctor again, and this time she was finally diagnosed with polio.

Mama lost faith in herself as a mother. She felt it was her fault her daughter had contracted the disease. My sister cried out in pain at all hours, frustrating my father and giving Awalbai even more of a reason to curse my mother. At the time, there was no vaccine or cure for polio and little was known about the illness. My mother would often cry with her at her crib side. Not knowing what to do, she'd give Yasmin prescribed sleeping pills to alleviate her pain and give the family some peace.

At this point, Mama had hidden a bottle of poison in her medicine cabinet. She contemplated suicide but feared if she were gone her children would suffer at the hands of a stepmother. Torn between her despair and her children's well-being, Mama sought advice from the dead.

Years earlier, one of her uncles shot himself. Mama, her brother, and a few other family members called to him through a type of Ouija board. They believe they reached him, and he spelled out how miserable he was on the other side and begged them never to contemplate suicide. After his spirit left, they decided to call on Mama's father for guidance. Mama told him once more of her unhappiness, of her sick daughter, and her loss of faith, but her father's reply was the same as it was when he was alive. He advised her once again to work on her marriage, that she would find happiness again. He instructed them not to contact him again, as it was disrupting his own spiritual journey.

Mama believed her father. She was desperate to find peace again, so she sought comfort in what had always made her strong—religion. Despite Awalbai's protest, Mama went to Jamat Khana every morning to pray, often bringing Yasmin and me along. As her faith strengthened, so did Yasmin. Eventually she was running and playing with me, though her early illness would have detrimental effects later in life. I began to share the same spiritual dedication as my mother, and like her I became very involved with the Muslim community. I think Mama found her purpose when she began to go to Jamat Khana again. She wanted to serve, not because she had to, as with her duties as matriarch, but because she wanted to.

Mama took joy in raising her children to adhere to and appreciate Muslim tradition and values as she did. And I loved seeing Mama so passionate about things again. She taught my sister and me how to sew and cook gourmet meals. I always looked forward to helping Mama in the kitchen. She was patient and always made sure I followed every step correctly. She'd often smile and laugh with me about things that had happened at school, not having to focus too much on the food since cooking was second nature to her. Even as an adult I'd always call Mama for cooking tips, and she'd always be happy to help me perfect my curry or biriyani. My father never stood in her way; though he did not share her dedication, he could see a change in her demeanor. Duties she normally dreaded were now taken in stride. She never really *enjoyed* them, but she believed her spirit was guiding her toward happiness, and with that she persevered.

As fate would have it, an opportunity for a senior position at the Motor Mart back in Kisumu reached my father. He applied with a very good reference from Kampala, landed the job, and rented another two-bedroom house in the neighboring village of Landi. The bicycle he rode to work for years was replaced with the family's first car, a Chevrolet van. Father began to become renowned in the motor business, with Mama's fame as a gifted tailor not to be outdone! My family was able to move to a house in the city, and soon it was time for my father to take the next step and open his own business, giving rise to Rainbow Garage in 1954. In the same building, Mama's own Rainbow Tailoring House was also born.

After a few years my family became one of the most prosperous in Kisumu. My father, always placing his priorities within the business, grew his legacy from one small garage to thirteen dealerships. During my childhood I had watched my parents struggle to make ends meet—now my father was able to afford to send me and my siblings to England for my education.

In 1955 Mama had my brother Nazir, and in 1964 my sister Neyleen was born. They had a posh childhood compared to mine, but Mama's insistence that they join her at Jamat Khana was just the same. My father also began to share in Mama's duty to faith—at our Jamat Khana he became the Mukhi (male leader) and Kamadia (male second leader), and he supported Mama when running for Mukhiani (female leader) and Kambadiani (female second leader). Together they ran the Jamat Khana every day for six years. They initiated all prayers during service, presided over weddings, births, deaths, and illness, and addressed many issues within the community, including poverty, crises, and even family feuds. Their positions were full-time jobs, but the love and respect they received from the imam community made it worthwhile.

My father's relocation to Kisumu also brought an end to the Khamisa family feud. My grandfather—an excellent businessman but a renowned partier—had lost his own fortune in a series of risky deals and indulgent spending. He humbled himself and asked my father for help, and the two were able to reconcile after nearly twenty years of estrangement. My father gave my grandfather a job at one of his thirteen businesses, so as the business grew, old relations blossomed as well. I loved getting to know my grandfather—rough around the edges, a bit crude at times, but possessed with a brilliant mind and infinite love for his grandchildren.

With my father and grandfather's reunion, Mama was also met with a new horde of in-laws. Mama was able to stay grounded when her family became rich, but my father's family was quite the contrary. They threw huge and elaborate parties, drank in excess, ate till they were fat, swore at each other, and did not attend Jamat Khana, though they faked their piety.

Of course, it is the matriarch's duty to serve her husband's family, and Mama did. Oh, but she did not like it one bit. She had an especially hard time catering to her mother and sisters-in-law, who believed her refusal to partake in their lifestyle was a sign of defiance and self-righteousness. Still, she cooked and cleaned for their family as well as her own, and once the women discovered her talent as a dressmaker, she became quite a busy house tailor as well. Again, my father was too busy growing his businesses to help, but Mama was more resilient than ever.

Even though she wasn't fond of her in-laws, she began to feel some pride as the matriarch. She'd host dinner parties and get-togethers as her mother had during her childhood, and always helped a family or friend in any way she could. She remembered every birthday on both sides of her family, and would send presents, cards, cakes, and dresses to someone almost every week. She made each family member feel important and loved, no matter the relationship. But that didn't really stop at family—she had a special place in her heart for everyone in the community. She always volunteered for community events, often cooking for huge banquets, weddings, and for those who may not have been able to afford food themselves. She and Father also donated money to orphanages in India and would continue to do so for the rest of their lives. She became an advocate for women's rights as well, and many women looked up to her for her role at Jamat Khana and the positions she held on various community councils. She truly wanted to improve the welfare of everyone around her. I remember telling her, "Mama, you take better care of the community's children than your own." But I wasn't complaining. I was proud.

My family lived a comfortable life for nearly twenty years. We excelled in our business and were well respected in the community. But despite the hardships we had been through, despite all my father had worked so hard to build and all the people my mother selflessly took under her wing, it all came crashing down.

In 1971 General Idi Amin overthrew the elected government of Milton Obote and declared himself president of Uganda, launching a ruthless eight-year regime in which an estimated three hundred thousand civilians were massacred. His goals were only to benefit Uganda's majority black population, and he blamed those of any other descent—especially Asians, who at the time were the backbone of the Ugandan economy—for milking the economy of its wealth. My family of Indian descent began to experience hate and racism like we had never experienced before. People who had once shaken hands with me or my father now wouldn't even look at us. On August 7, 1972, Idi Amin finally made the shocking declaration that anyone who was not black—mainly Asians, Indians, and Pakistanis—must leave the country within ninety days.

Some ninety thousand people were forced from their homes in Uganda. On the way to the airport, the new government set up dozens of checkpoints where families would be stripped of their money, jewelry, clothing, and precious heirlooms. Many arrived in England, Canada, and Europe with nothing to begin a new life with, not even a coat to shield them from the harsh winter.

Mama's maiden family, as well as my in-laws, became refugees overnight. Idi Amin's declaration gave them little time to prepare, and they had no choice but to leave their home and split up. The family she had tried so hard to keep together and acknowledge every birthday, wedding, birth, and death was now spread to places she'd never even dreamed of going—Los Angeles, the United Kingdom, Halifax, among others. Mama made dresses for all her nieces, cousins, and sisters-in-law within the short ninety days before they were all forced from their home—a final gift as they left all they knew in Kenya, each stitch representing the promise of resilience and love from my mother's own needle.

Mama's family, as well as my own, was still in Kenya, just east of Uganda. But as our family was involved in the exodus in Uganda, we feared Kenya would suffer the same fate. It was resolved that our family would leave the country and head west voluntarily before we were forced out.

Since I had studied in England and was the oldest son, I was the first to relocate to Vancouver, Canada, in 1964. Before leaving I had to sell the family business back home, which took nearly two years, but I was able to rent a small home in Vancouver from the profits.

But after learning that business opportunities were substantially better in America, I decided to resettle again, this time in Seattle, Washington. I became a part-owner of a manufacturer of specialty bread mixes and bought a good-size home. In 1976 Mama's family as well as my own came to stay with me in Seattle.

In 1976 we were the first Ismaili Muslims to settle in Seattle. There was no Jamat Khana or Muslim community, and Mama, whose life revolved around Jamat Khana and daily practice, was at a loss. When I told her about the main Jamat Khana I had attended while in Vancouver, she decided she wanted to live there. I obliged and we found her a home in Canada, and she, my father, and my sister Neyleen moved there.

When she first arrived in Vancouver, Mama was eager to join the growing Muslim community who had immigrated as refugees like us. She attended Jamat Khana early every morning as she had in Kenya, but this time with a zeal that teetered on the brink of obsession. Nothing and no one could stop her. If the family traveled anywhere with Mama, the first thing we had to do was find the nearest Jamat Khana and work our schedule around prayer time. It didn't matter if it snowed or hailed or if she or one of her children was sick. Even when she was dying Mama never, *ever* missed daily prayer and meditation, with exception of her last few days.

She made many friends those few months we spent in Vancouver—she always had a smile despite the circumstances, and so many people were drawn to her energy and dedication to find a new normal in a strange and foreign country. Mama began to learn by trial and error the ways of the West, her adventurous spirit thrilled with the new and exciting opportunities that awaited her family, comforted knowing our faith would guide us toward eventual success.

But after a short while she decided to head to Seattle again to help my growing family adjust. I was occupied with my business, and my wife had just had our second child—our only son, Tariq. Mama busied herself cooking and watching after the kids, but, as before, she yearned for an Ismaili community to be a part of.

When more Ismailis began to migrate to Seattle in search of a promising life, Mama jumped at the opportunity to host them as they searched for their own home and vocation. We had a large house with four bedrooms and a finished basement, so room was never an issue. Just like her own mother, who had never turned down a chance to be hospitable, Mama was soon cooking, cleaning, and charming a home of complete strangers—though she considered them "brothers" and "sisters." I had a few connections with Seattle businesses and corporations, so I would often help early settlers find new careers and occupations. But Mama would help them get accustomed to a new Western lifestyle—she taught many how to prepare Western-style dishes, how to shop in Western malls and grocery stores, and how to ride public transit. Word of Mama's kindness spread, and more refugees sought our support. At one point there were so many Ismailis staying at our home that we dubbed it the "Khamisa motel." But the hosting helped Mama find her purpose—and her joy—again.

In 1976, as this new community began to grow, Mama took it upon herself to help organize the first ever Seattle Ismaili Jamat Khana in the basement of our home. On Fridays and Sundays when the community would join us at our makeshift Jamat Khana, Mama would prepare the basement for prayer and meditation and bake *seero*, a sweet rice-like dish made with five ingredients that specify special attributes of living a pure spiritual life. A friend of mine and I served as the laity clerics and led the group through three prayers; *ginans*, or hymns with spiritual guidance and predictions; and inspirational readings, or *firmans*, from the Aga Khan, the Ismaili secular and spiritual head. Mama would choose the *ginans* and *firmans* to be included in the service each week and often conducted her own prayers, careful to choose ones that would relate to and inspire those who were struggling with their transition. She led her own meditation groups as well and gained many disciples throughout the years, including myself.

Our humble makeshift Jamat Khana became the epicenter of the Seattle Ismaili community, and soon more and more Ismailis were determined to pack themselves into our basement for prayer. Although Mama never turned away someone seeking the services of the Jamat Khana, we knew this wouldn't do. With the help of the community we rented a space exclusively for the Jamat Khana in the community room of one of the cleric's condominiums. With more room away from our own personal living space, we began to meet every day for prayer and meditation, a schedule more typical for an Ismaili Jamat Khana. As the Jamat Khana's attendees grew, the rented community room was soon swapped for a larger office space. Mama was always sure to make enough tea and cookies for everyone, every day.

Mama returned to Vancouver after establishing the Jamat Khana in Seattle, but today her legacy has become a proper free-standing Jamat Khana with over a thousand worshippers. She felt her duty in Seattle had been fulfilled, and her heart had always been in Canada. Up until she was no longer able to drive, Mama arrived at Vancouver's enormous Jamat Khana at three o'clock every morning to serve tea and cookies to worshippers and returned again for evening prayer. She even had her own key to the Jamat Khana since she usually arrived before anyone else.

During the latter part of her life, Mama served her family, friends, community, and God with passion and devotion. Her duties were never met with dread, as they had been before when she was a young wife in a new family. She found happiness knowing she was doing all she could with every ounce of her spirit to improve the lives around her. And she took so much pride watching her own family grow! When her own children began to have kids, and our children began families of their own, Mama was there every step of the way. She'd help the moms-to-be prepare for the daunting yet exciting arrival, she was with them during and after birth, and she always offered to help with cooking, cleaning, and babysitting. If she wasn't there, Mama was always a phone call away with advice and a listening ear. She made sure to acknowledge every birthday, no matter the distance between her and her grandchildren and great-grandchildren—she wanted everyone to feel special and loved. And the morals and values she held throughout her life—the ones that made her resilient, compassionate, and peaceful—she was careful to instill within each child.

With that, I know Mama never really left us, at least not in spirit. Every time I forgive, offer a helping hand, or stand up against the wrong in this world, there is Mama. Her heart lives on within the children she helped raise, the friends who confided in her, and all of those she inspired.

Mama did not end a war, world hunger, or poverty. She did not build a billion-dollar corporation or change the nation through government policies. But as a leader, Mama is my greatest inspiration. As matriarch, mother, business owner, and spiritual and community leader, my mother exemplified mastery in all three components of a satyagrahi leader. She was more than a tailor; she was a servant to God, her family, and her community, demonstrating competency in her fields of endeavor beyond her career. She was always so quick to lend a helping hand to whoever came to her with problems, whether they be personal or societal. She did all in her power to make a contribution toward the betterment of her community, mastering the second element found among satyagrahi leaders. And above all, Mama's unshakeable spiritual and moral strength gave her the power to overcome her own trials, a trait she made sure to pass on to her own children and to those who came to her for guidance. She was a light in the dark, but she believed everyone had the same light within them—it just needed to be sparked.

After her death, Mama's family, friends, and loved ones came together to share their most memorable and inspiring stories of Mama. With everyone's contribution, we allowed hope and happiness to shine through the gloom of our loss.

"Lovely to see the family all connected, and hopefully will remain so!

"It made me sad not to have been able to spend the last remaining days close to Mama. However, I found comfort in the fact that in the last several years, during our visit to North America, I was able to spend four to six weeks every year with her and Neyleen, who had been taking care of Mama for more than five years. We ate breakfast, lunch, and most dinners together and talked and told stories until bedtime.

"My favorite was always lunch with her. She would ask me what I wanted to eat (usual Mama question), and I would ask for a cheese sandwich like the ones she ate every day. Let me tell you all—she made the best cheese sandwich! During the last visit, she was having trouble cutting cucumbers and cheese, so I made the sandwich using the very same ingredients (under her watchful eye), but it just didn't taste the same. So the next day I prepared all the ingredients and had Mama build it . . . guess what? It tasted so good! Mama had magic in her fingers. She showed her love through food—I believe all of us would agree. She spoiled everyone rotten with her cooking."

—Shelina, daughter-in-law

"My memory of Remy Auntie is that she always took an interest in what was going on in our lives and how we were getting on versus focusing on herself. She was warm, always giving and hard working—she got things done. She practiced all her life the same mantra Nike chose as their tagline—Just Do It!

"As a testament to her reach and impact—Aziz Bhaloo, who was from Kisumu and was president of Ismaili Council Canada—called me last week when he heard about Remy Auntie. He spoke so glowingly about her."

—Farouk Ahamed, nephew

"I am sitting here at the airport and thinking about the last few days and how they unfolded. I was humbled by the visitors that came to see Mum while she was in hospital and hospice. I was blown away by the number of phone calls and the words that came out from most of the conversations we had. All we heard was 'what a person,' 'straight to heaven,' 'she had done so much for us,' and a lot of insight on her service and work for which we had no knowledge of before. Yet we knew she had served all her life.

"I began to think about how I as a person could live my life like she did and accumulate what we call spiritual currency, and just be a good human being."

—Nazir, second son

"The story I would like to share is from when I was mukhiani of student majlis. Mama really wanted to come down for my majlis, but it wasn't working out for us to drive up to get her that weekend. So, Mama, being the mischievous grandmother that she was, decided that she would make some food for the majlis and behind everyone's back made her way to the greyhound station and showed up in Seattle! She merely left a note for Neyleen and took off, worrying everyone! In true Mama fashion, she made it to the majlis, and it was a wonderful surprise. I feel grateful to have had Mama be a part of it and will always remember her spunk and hope to be at least half as cool as she was in her eighties!"

—Soraiya, granddaughter

"It has been wonderful to read all these amazing stories of mama and connect with family. It has been difficult for me to contribute, as it is still so raw. It is still so hard to believe she is gone, as her loss is still so hard. But she is at peace, I am sure of that, and we are all so blessed to have been loved by her.

"Mama was a beautiful soul who had such a special relationship with so many, and we are all blessed to be part of that group. I have many beautiful memories of Mama, but the most special for me is when she came to help me with the birth of all three of my children. Making me catlo (a rich mixture of nuts, molasses, grains, oil, and other nourishing ingredients) and heating it up for me every morning. I was so sick when I was pregnant with my daughter, so she came and took care of me at the age of eighty and then came again for my daughter's baptism. She cooked meals and froze them so I would not have to worry about food after the babies came. My daughter's middle name is Remy in honor of Mama. My daughter just turned six in March, and we FaceTimed with Mama and Neyleen during her birthday celebration. Mama was able to sing her 'Happy Birthday'—I will forever hold that moment close to my heart.

"In the last few years she was a source of strength and support for me as I was going through a rough patch. She listened with patience, and the words 'I love you' and 'I am here for you' always gave me a sense of peace.

"You will always remain in our hearts, Mama, and thank you for your love, your prayers and your support.

"Miss and love you so much."

—Tasreen, granddaughter

"Everyone's prayers and stories have been incredibly beautiful and deeply touching. I am in tears. When my family had lost everything and my parents made their move to Mityana in poverty, Remi Aunty, among many other compassionate gestures, made some of the most beautiful dresses for Azra, Azmina, and me (I can still picture them). I even remember, at the age of seven, what it felt like to be in these gorgeous outfits that were clearly made with love. This was her way of helping out my mother, her sister.

"Thank you, Remi Aunty, for your kindness when my mom needed it the most. Having three children of my own I know what that support meant to her.

"May your soul rest in eternal peace!"

—Afrose, niece

## Question to Ponder

The main question to ask here is, "Who has impacted my life in a profound way and has made me who I am?" That understanding can go a long way in helping you make better and more spiritually aligned decisions that are in concert with the universal laws. Often when I am stymied on a decision or an action I ask, "What would Mama do?" and often the right answer shows up even though she has passed. Who is that person in your life?

# CONCLUSION

Now that you have almost finished the book and learned about these brilliant role models, what is the big takeaway?

For starters, it's important to notice that all the examples of satyagrahi leaders come from different backgrounds, different genders, different nationalities, different races, and different faiths. They also possess different strengths and have succeeded in an exemplary way in their individual careers, inventing viable and affordable solutions to societal challenges while espousing and spreading strong moral, ethical, and spiritual values. Another obvious thing to notice is that they all have different strengths but have honed those strengths over a number of years, staying steadfast to their missions and looking at failures and disappointments as positive stepping-stones to their vision and mission. These role models have used failure to further their resiliency and strengthen their positive qualities and beliefs. So the two big lessons here are to understand that true leadership comes from: (1) intimately understanding and reflecting on our strengths; and (2) selecting role models from whom we can learn and draw encouragement. In that way, we each can become a satyagrahi leader. To do that requires understanding the self, selecting role models, and reflecting on how we can embody our strengths with fortitude, like the leaders

I highlighted. Even though most of the chosen leaders went through a calamity that inspired a new direction in their life of service, you do not need to necessarily go through a calamity to make a change. As humans we all get hard hits, which is the Universe's way of nudging us toward our spiritual purpose, which resides in service of others. We all are born with a spiritual purpose, and once we find that purpose our lives are happier, more meaningful, healthier, and a way for us to leave a lasting legacy.

## Understanding the Self

While threats to the environment and individual, family, and community life have existed as long as humans have existed, it is questionable whether they have existed at the scale and with the speed we witness today. Some of the systematic, overarching threats to global peace, stability, and thriving include:

climate degradation

threats to democracy and civil society

income and wealth disparities that do not budge over time

global challenges to immigration

sexual abuse against children and women as exposed by the #MeToo movement

modern slavery and trafficking

genocides that have plagued our species with such force in the last century

These threats are fueled and perpetuated by self-centered interests and result in myopic policies that polarize and separate humankind, while those in power are largely insulated from the fallout of these threats. What can disrupt the human tendency to marginalize those with whom we believe we have little in common is that we instead lead all global citizens in productive, life-affirming ways that contribute to a thriving and more integrated world community.

**We need leaders who can lead with self-understanding, work, social and spiritual competency, and the fortitude to contribute positively to the world.** To become changemakers for the difficult times we find ourselves in today, tomorrow's leaders must embody the three competencies (professional, social, and spiritual). The third competency *in particular* may be the one that powers the most creative solutions. Unlike the two other forms of expertise, spiritual competence is not discussed at length in business management journals, and "success" is not typically defined by how leaders manifest their deepest beliefs about spiritual truths. If innovation is defined as a new reality that reframes the way we think about something, then the teachings of the world's religions' major founders were highly innovative. Those teachings have changed the way people think about themselves, their families, and their communities. Innovation can come in the form of business, social, or, I believe, spiritual innovation. For example, Jesus of Nazareth and Siddhartha Gautama were powerful precisely because they challenged the ethos of the day and provided a new set of principles to live by. They were clearly innovators. One could argue that the most well-known leaders across history have either been conquerors of the external world (e.g., Genghis Khan) or of the internal world (e.g., Laozi) or both (e.g., Muhammed). Because we live in a world that has largely been conquered by technology and where national borders often do not separate people from interacting, the next "place" humans can conquer is internal. Perhaps it's for this reason that the fourteenth Dalai Lama has created bridges between the once-esoteric practices of Tibetan Buddhism and those of Western science because he intuited that if we want to create peace globally, we need to use different paradigms to understand our lived experiences. In his view, the "clash" between religion and science—or between any two worldviews—is not inevitable, but there has to be a system by which these two worldviews interact. We believe that satyagrahi leaders teach us innovative ways to be leaders, not least in the realm of the moral, ethical, spiritual, and religious.

I highlighted the leaders in this book because they have personally influenced the way I understand being a changemaker. I was not born to be a leader, but I am lucky to have had amazing role models to show me other ways of living beyond the self that benefit others and bring us closer to truth, compassion, and equality. And while I was not born a leader, these lifelong influences sparked a desire to become a changemaker when my life fell apart after my son died. We all have situations that could spark us to become the leaders that our families and communities and maybe the world need us to be. But if we do not know our strengths or have role models that embody the three forms of expertise, what will inspire us to turn difficult or even tragic circumstances into healing, into greater integrity, for the benefit of others?

## Identifying Our Strengths

To identify your strengths, there are many different models of assessment, such as StrengthsFinder, Myers Briggs, and others. Many of you already know what your strengths are. The tool for understanding one's strengths is less important than the fact that you select your assessment tool and get clarity about your positive qualities. Gandhi and Winston Churchill had very different strengths, but both were extraordinarily competent in their strengths and used them in ways that changed history. We all have the requisite strengths to be a satyagrahi leader, and the main purpose of getting clarity on your strengths is to continue to build on them.

For example, one tool that helped me get more clarity of my strengths was from a book called *Strengths Based Leadership*, by Tom Rath and Barry Conchie. When I took the StrengthsFinder test many years ago, I discovered from the thirty-minute test that my five strengths were as follows: I was an achiever, I believed in the connectedness of all things, I was futuristic, I was positive, and I was responsible.

Since then I have continued to hone my strengths with other tools and life experiences. There is much to learn from the outcomes we create every day in our lives. I knew much of this resided in my own character and personality, but the test was a good validation. No doubt you will make a similar discovery of your character and personality when you pursue discovering your strengths.

**Ultimately, for leaders to address our daunting challenges, they will need super-competency not only in their chosen professions—as taught by most institutions of higher learning—but also equal competence in social transformation and a strong adherence to moral, ethical, and spiritual values.** In other words, we must train our future leaders to tackle complex societal challenges by learning skills beyond their chosen university majors or fields of endeavor. We must understand and teach a broader understanding of the true calling of leadership. In doing so we should also ask ourselves, Do we live and demonstrate the following triad of competencies?

1. **Do we possess competence in our chosen fields, whether in engineering, law, medicine, business, architecture, education, nonprofit work, justice, government, mothers, fathers, citizens, or other fields of endeavor that make our global society and economy work?** We must strive to create a global society that works for all. That is the best security and a precursor to world peace. An academic resume alone, however, does not fulfill the job description for tomorrow's leaders.

2. **Do we have equal competence in tackling societal issues that make their respective communities a better place to live?** This requires going beyond just filling individual bank

accounts to fulfilling the wider needs of the community—to love
your neighbor as you love yourself. Nonprofit organizations, civic
clubs, and other groups require leaders at all levels.

3. **Do we have a moral, ethical, and spiritual competence
that embraces truth, empathy, compassion, love, service,
and community?** Spiritual competence does not necessarily
translate to adhering to a certain faith or religion. The spirit is the
voice that speaks beyond our own, guiding us to make the best
decision based on our personal morals. These values—like nature
and gravity—will always prevail. While all faiths teach these universal spiritual values, few leaders adhere to them.

Once you have identified your strengths, then the task going forward
is to continue to build on them through your research, your life lessons,
your readings, or in conversation with others.

## Selecting and Reflecting on Role Models

One key to becoming a satyagrahi leader is to consciously select role models who can shape *how you think about leadership*. I have selected a few in
this book, but over the years there have been many who have helped me
successfully navigate my challenges. I will describe their influences on me,
both those who are profiled in this book as well as others who have made
an indelible mark on how I lead my life.

I will provide an example: I had to interrupt my studies in England
to take over a family business in Kenya, as my father had a heart condition and could not continue to work. Having passed my intermediate
exam in finance and secured the first place out of eighteen thousand
students with a passing rate of only 18 percent, my professor Dr. Harvey
was very disappointed that I had dropped out and did not continue to
my final exam. I had to explain that as the oldest son in a Muslim family

I was the surrogate father, and my mother had put the guilt trip on me by asking, "What is more important—your education or your father's health?" In any case, I did well with the business, doubled its profits in eighteen months, and added a subsidiary On a subsequent visit to see Dr. Harvey, he asked me how I was doing. I responded that I was doing well and we were still the number one auto dealership in my small town, but I was concerned as to whether we could stay there because of increasing competition from other auto manufacturers. At this point he said to me, "I am very disappointed with you." Of course, I was in tears, as he was like a God to me and I had been his star student. With my chin in my lap I eked out, "Why, Dr. Harvey, are you disappointed in me?" He said, "I am disappointed in you because you are looking over your shoulder to see who is catching up to you—what I want to know is, what are you doing to catch the person in front of you?" The truth is, there is always someone in front of you, and that is why it is crucial to have role models. Wow—what a wise lesson! I was doing business in a small town in Western Kenya, and since then I have never looked back over my shoulder and instead successfully advanced to bigger and better challenges, including emigrating and doing business in America—a long cry from the small town in Kenya.

My own lessons from each of these leaders are summarized below as examples to help you reflect on and build your strengths.

## Chapter 2: Ignatius of Loyola

From the Proverbs 15:33 we learn: "Humility comes before honor" (NIV). Ignatius is a good example of learning that from a misfortune. Not all of us make the right decision when we are hit hard. Ignatius was able to do that. My own feeling is that we all have defining moments in our lives, and if we are able to make the right decision at these junctures, we literally manifest a miracle in ourselves and others. That was the case in my life when I lost my only son. In every tragedy there is a spark of clarity—Ignatius, too, was able to see a spark in his own tragedy that helped him build the largest and oldest (over five hundred years) educational system in the world! Every saint has suffered the dark night of the soul, and Ignatius is a very good example of that.

## Chapter 3: His Highness Prince Karim Aga Khan IV

In terms of my own evolution he has been a huge exemplar for the work that I have done and continue to do. One of the biggest gifts that came from his sage advice very early in my life was that "your spiritual and material life are equally important." The integral word in this statement is "equally." Sure, we are spiritual beings in a human form, but this advice encourages us to respect the duality of our human life and our spiritual life. This has helped me tremendously in my growth over the years, as from a very young age I gave equal emphasis both to my career and my spiritual life. That meant that I would pray and meditate daily, was always involved with serving my community as a volunteer, and simultaneously worked to further my chosen career in business. If I am reading a book on business, I am at the same time reading a book on strengthening my spiritual resiliency—a practice I have continued until today. The big payoff was that, when I lost my son tragically, what saved me was not my education in mathematics and finance but my spiritual foundation. I learned that in life you are going to get challenges your intellect will not be able to solve even if you have a double PhD, or you'll get challenges that your heart will not be able to heal, but by the same token there are *no* problems you are going to face in your life that your spirit cannot solve or heal. I believe I am a good example of that. This is well documented in my book, *The Secrets of the Bulletproof Spirit: How to Bounce Back from Life's Hardest Hits,* coauthored with Jillian Quinn. There is much wisdom and inspiration to receive from this amazing exemplar, and you can learn more about this from researching AKDN. org and other websites.

## Chapter 4: Mata Amritanandamayi (Amma)

The courage and faith of Amma, with only a sixth-grade education and born into a poor fisherman family in the Kerala region of South India, and her amazing accomplishments truly are mind boggling and defy reality. She is known by her devotees for selfless love and compassion. (Note that earlier I mentioned critiques of her leadership, but, as is true with all leaders, no one is without fault or critique. It's the perseverance despite personal faults that makes these leaders great.) Her life has been dedicated to alleviating the pain of the poor and those suffering physically and emotionally. While Amma is widely regarded as one of India's foremost spiritual leaders, Amma says that her religion is love. She does not ask audiences to change their religion, only to contemplate the essential principles of their own faith and to try to live accordingly. Her philosophy, simply stated, is, "Where there is true love, anything is effortless."

What I have learned from this enlightened saint and soul with immeasurable energy to heal the world is her faith. From Matthew 17:20 we learn, "Verily I say unto you, If ye have faith as a grain of mustard seed, ye shall say unto this mountain, Remove hence to yonder place; and it shall remove; and nothing shall be impossible unto you" (King James Version). Amma exemplifies this in a real and convincing way. Nothing seems impossible for her. Faith is the ability to believe in something that is not evident or provable. Often, we are mired by indecision based on our intellectual analysis of what is possible or not possible, especially when we find ourselves in what the Tibetan Buddhist called a *Bardo*. A Bardo is "a transition or gap between the completion of one situation and the onset of another," from *bar*—"in between" and *do*—"suspended," or "thrown." There are many Bardos in life: birth, adolescence, school graduations, first jobs, getting fired, marriage, divorce, and the normal ups and downs of life. Of course, the supreme of all Bardos is death. Bardos are where all of us navigate serious challenges and hurdles in our lives, and in so doing, we learn important lessons to spur our growth and spiritual evolution.

At these Bardos in life, it feels like crossing a chasm. The intellect, most affiliated with the first competency of leaders, says there is no way you can cross this chasm in one step. On the other hand, your unwavering faith inspires you in the affirmative to not only cross the chasm in one step, but when you get to the other side you find yourself on higher ground! Tibetan Buddhists spend their entire lives building their faith so they know that when they die, they can step out of samsara (birth–death–rebirth) into nirvana (enlightenment and unity with the source). Amma is one embodiment of living in faith—and from her I have learned to develop and further strengthen my faith and to believe in what cannot be seen. What may seem impossible to achieve is indeed possible through the unwavering faith of your spirit.

## Chapter 5: Elie Weisel

World history would be a lot different without the contribution of Elie Wiesel, who taught us that the opposite of hatred was not love but indifference. He was a champion for speaking out on injustice and did seminal work in making sure the atrocities of the Holocaust are never forgotten and to make sure this never happens again. Elie also had a high level of compassion and empathy and promoted forgiveness. In a documentary entitled *The Power of Forgiveness*—one of a half-dozen stories on forgiveness, including mine—Elie is shown addressing the German Bundestag in Bonn. He is extremely eloquent and thanks the German government for all they have done for Jews since the Holocaust. But he is also very animated and forceful when he tells the German legislators that the one thing they have *not* done is to ask for the forgiveness of the Jewish people.

He wonders aloud, "Why don't you ask for our forgiveness?" A week later, as a result of this address, the then Chancellor of Germany Helmut Kohl flew to Tel Aviv, addressed the Israeli Knesset, and publicly asked for their forgiveness. Understanding the power of forgiveness in my own life to promote and manifest peace and a better society, I clearly resonate with Elie and was able to learn from him that the macro-level of forgiveness is possible. I believe forgiveness can literally change the world.

Another one of my favorite quotes is from his Nobel lecture, when he said, "Mankind must remember that peace is not God's gift to his creatures, it is our gift to each other." The importance of hope is that it allows us to believe in human nature and the fact that the power of compassion and forgiveness indeed can heal us at both the individual and societal levels. I have been passionately pursuing this practice for the last twenty-five years of my life. My sincere prayer is that the good Lord has granted him eternal peace in heaven, as he definitely is very deserving of that and has earned my deep and sincere respect.

The most important lesson that I learned from Elie is his tireless and selfless passion and effort to eradicate indifference in our lives. No one is perfect—we as humans are all fallible. It is critical that we develop this empathy for all sentient beings with whom we share our beautiful planet. This makes forgiveness possible and eradicates indifference and judgments. In the words of another great favorite master of mine, Jalāl ad-Dīn Muhammad Rūmī:

"All the children of Abraham are like the fingers of one hand, when you cause harm to one finger and you don't think you are hurting the other fingers you do not deserve to be called human."

## Chapter 6: Mubarak Awad

Mubarak is a close personal friend; I sometimes jokingly refer to him as a "brother from a different mother." As you read in the book, he has a powerful story of compassion and commitment to nonviolence. This meant that it was not difficult for us to see we were indeed cut from the same fabric, although our background is totally different: he is a Palestinian-born Christian, and I am a Kenyan-born Sufi Muslim with Eastern heritage. Despite that, we quickly saw that we indeed were divinely brought together and would do good work together.

I met him for the first time in 1998 when the National Youth Advocate Program was celebrating its twentieth anniversary. It was a five-day conference in Columbus, Ohio, where NYAP is headquartered, and they had five keynote speakers, one for each day. I spoke on the fourth day, and Desmond Tutu, another champion of nonviolence and forgiveness, was the closing speaker. So I was in good company! My talk was well received, as NYAP works with underserved and disenfranchised youth in nine states and provides a plethora of exemplary services to these youth and their families. So the audience of primarily social workers was extremely positively moved by my story, and Mubarak later asked me to create a program for his organization for youth—many of whom were street smart and had a violent history. This was a dream come true for me. In my story, I realized there were victims at both ends of the gun, and the foundation I had created in memory of my son essentially was a preventive effort to make sure youth do not fall prey to gangs, violence, crime, drugs, alcohol, and weapons, as did the young man who killed my son. Here Mubarak was offering me an opportunity to create an intervention program for youth who were already offenders, often gang involved, and in many cases, still living lives of crime and violence. I saw this population as one of victims, even while they may have been perpetrators.

I worked hand-in-glove with Mubarak and the senior team at NYAP to create a program for this population called CANEI—an acronym for Constant and Never-Ending Improvement—a good mantra for this population based on the philosophy that "I will be a better person tomorrow than I am today and continue to improve every single day." I am sure you will agree that this motto can apply to all of us! So the CANEI program was launched in 2000 with three pillars:

(1) Spirituality: understanding that transformation lives in the spirit from my own experience—not religion but an existential reliance on our innate internal spirit, which guides and helps us navigate the challenges of lives in a positive way
(2) Restorative justice where youth are encouraged to take responsibility for their actions, ask forgiveness of their victims, forgive themselves, and redeem themselves by changing their behaviors forever and helping other youth not to follow in their previous footsteps
(3) Literacy with a focus on reading, writing, and arithmetic, as many entered the CANEI program with none of these skills

So essentially, CANEI was designed to work with Head through the literacy pillar, with Heart through the restorative justice pillar, and with Spirit through the spirituality pillar. We saw this as a holistic, humane, and comprehensive program working on all aspects of what makes us human. With the grace of God and hard work, the program delivered some incredible results much like TKF and today has grown into a much-enhanced and a premier NYAP program serving youth in many of NYAP's states. Mubarak and I stay in close contact as we continue to discuss constant and never-ending improvements from the lessons we learn from our constituents in TKF and CANEI. Thank you, Mubarak, for your leadership, role modeling, support, and friendship over these many years. You have been a true inspiration to me and a co-satyagrahi leader.

## Chapter 7: Daisaku Ikeda

Soka Gakkai, rooted in Buddhist philosophy, is a global organization that has grown under the leadership of Daisaku Ikeda, who introduced the concept of a culture of peace. He is a champion of peace and has committed his entire life to promote peace in the world. He is a giant in the peace movement, and there is much to learn from this wise sage who has authored many books and founded many nonprofit organizations. The central tenet of Ikeda's thought, and of Buddhism, is the fundamental sanctity of life, a value which Ikeda sees as the key to lasting peace and human happiness. In his view, global peace relies ultimately on a self-directed transformation within the life of the individual, rather than on societal or structural reforms alone. This idea is expressed most succinctly in a passage in his best-known work, *The Human Revolution*, Ikeda's novelization of the Soka Gakkai's history and ideals: "A great human revolution in just a single individual will help achieve a change in the destiny of a nation, and, further, will enable a change in the destiny of all humankind." I find a lot of power in this last statement, as I have seen and experienced that a single person can indeed create shifts in humanity. We have seen this in Gandhi, Nelson Mandela, and the people featured in this book. There are many other unsung heroes in most communities working toward peace. We all want peace—peace within us, peace in our families, and peace in our communities. But peace is a proactive effort we must all collectively work at. The portal for me to achieve peace was forgiveness. My trilogy starts with a very dark genesis of the devastating murder of my only son, *From Murder to Forgiveness.* I followed that with a sequel, *From Forgiveness to Fulfillment,* as the work I have done in the aftermath of my son's death has been very meaningful and fulfilling. This I followed with *From Fulfillment to Peace.* My last book of the trilogy was inspired by the below quote I wrote in my journal:

"Sustained good will creates friendship, sustained friendship creates trust, sustained trust creates empathy, and sustained empathy creates peace."

But often I am asked, How do you extend goodwill to the person who murdered your child? I answer, you do that through forgiveness. As it is evident it worked for me and my family, what I believe is a miracle is that it worked for him and his family, and it can work for you and your family. Indeed, it can work for Israel and Palestine, North and South Korea, Afghanistan, Syria, Iran, Iraq, and America. It can work for the planet. Peace is possible. How do I know that? Because I am at peace!

I wanted to feature Daisaku Ikeda, as it shows what a single person can achieve in a lifetime when they are dedicated resolutely to a cause. This is in the hope that it inspires many, including myself, to continue steadfastly and dedicatedly in the pursuit of one's mission to create a better, more peaceful world. Indeed, peacemaking and peacebuilding are proactive efforts, and I am much inspired by Ikeda and his amazing accomplishments over his lifetime. Here again is a champion satyagrahi leader.

## Chapter 8: Wilma Mankiller

While I was not born in North America, I have learned much from the sage wisdom of the Native Americans. One of my favorite books is *Black Elk Speaks*, by John G. Neihardt, an American poet and writer. I have learned there is much wisdom in aboriginal cultures but, due to westernization, we have lost the wisdom and rituals of those cultures. For example, the love they have for Earth, if emulated, could have averted many climate challenges. Wilma Mankiller expresses many of these qualities. She tirelessly continued to improve the conditions of her Cherokee tribe despite her own ill health. As we learned in Chapter 8, she committed herself to community development projects and organizations, establishing more tribally owned businesses, improving infrastructure, constructing new schools, job-training centers, and health clinics, and, perhaps most importantly, redefining the relationship between the tribes and the US government. She improved federal trade negotiations under the US federal policy of Native American self-determination, which refers to the social movements, legislation, and beliefs by which tribes within the United States exercise self-governance and decision-making on issues that affect their people. Mankiller helped set a mutual understanding and respect between the Cherokee Nation and the United States that holds to this day.

The important lesson for me was Mankiller's putting herself second to her community and tribe. There was no selfishness in her, and she truly was an exemplary leader who dedicated her life to service and her community. Even more, she impacted other tribes' relationships with the US government and the US government's understanding of itself in relationship to Native American tribes. She reminds me of a quote that I mentioned earlier, attributed to Rabindranath Tagore:

"I slept and dreamt that life was joy. I awoke and saw that life was service. I acted and behold, service was joy."

## Chapter 9: Kazuo Inamori

Inamori is an amazing human being, hugely successful entrepreneur, Zen Buddhist priest, societal hero, and founder of the Kyoto Prize. I think it is worthy to repeat the following quote:

"Those worthy of the Kyoto Prize will be people who have, as have we at Kyocera, worked humbly and devotedly, sparing no effort to seek perfection in their chosen professions. They will be individuals who are sensitive to their own human fallibility and who thereby hold a deeply rooted reverence for excellence. Their achievements will have contributed substantially to the cultural, scientific, and spiritual betterment of mankind. Perhaps most importantly, they will be people who have sincerely aspired through the fruits of their labors to bring true happiness to humanity."

Truly an exemplary satyagrahi leader, he has been a true inspiration to me and so many others around the world. I was fortunate to serve on the Kyoto Prize Board for the San Diego Chapter and traveled to Japan to attend the main ceremony. Inamori's humility is striking in spite of his incredible wealth and success in business. You do not see the combination of true humility and material success very often. His resilience and persistence are qualities that I revere and strive to develop. His commitment to create a better and happier society is what I believe we were put on earth to do. This reminds me of a quote widely attributed to Albert Schweitzer:

"I don't know what your destiny will be, but one thing I know: the only ones among you who will be really happy are those who will have sought and found how to serve."

## Chapter 10: Remy Khamisa

A mother is probably the most important person in one's life. They gave us birth and, ideally, nurtured us and stood by our side through thick and thin. In many ways, although this book was in my head for a couple of years, it finally came to the forefront after my mother passed on April 28, 2017. I started writing the book in beautiful Maui a few months later. I learned many important lessons from my mother over the years; she was always the rock of my life. Having lost my elder sister, then my father, and then my only son, I thought I would do well with the passing of my mother. Not so! This has been very hard, as she was my foundation and I lost that firm footing in her passing. It has been three years, but I still miss her so much. My savior has been my younger sister Neyleen, who was her caregiver for the last several years. Neyleen did an awesome job taking care of our mum, who was able to live in her home her entire life except for the last ten days of her life spent in a hospital and hospice. Ever since she passed, I talk to my sister Neyleen every week, and she often consoles me by sharing the stories of my mum. Here are some examples.

For a start, Mum was devoutly spiritual and went to Jamat Khana twice a day, never missing a day in her life. Sufis meditate from 4:00 a.m. to 5:00 a.m. (a practice I have continued since I learned meditation at age twenty from one of Mum's spiritual teachers), and she always got to Jamat Khana at 3:00 a.m. to make tea and coffee and provide snacks for the earlier worshipers. She did not miss many days except toward the end of her life. We also pray again in the evening, and she never missed the evening payers. She was very active in leading prayers and served as a volunteer in many capacities for women, youth, and the poor in our community. I remember teasing her by saying, "Mama, you take better care of our community kids than your own, but I am not complaining—I am very proud of you." I think my commitment to serve and my willpower comes from her. I was amazed at the commitment she made to serve her community and her family, and that never faltered. She also was a very positive person. I remember that whenever I had a hard hit or was bruised or injured, her attitude was, "Everything happens for the best, and it could have been a lot worse. So God saved you from a much larger hit or catastrophe by subjecting you to a minor fender-bender." My mother had a tough life and marriage, having to serve two mothers-in-law and a grandmother-in-law, neither very compassionate nor considerate. She, however, understood that her duty was to her family. She never faltered and always rose to the occasion.

My mum was very talented, although she only had a grade school education. She was a talented seamstress, an amazing cook, a respected and coveted social worker, and an exemplary mother, wife, and grandmother. She consistently stayed in contact with her six siblings and their children, never forgetting a holiday or a birthday. She was a woman of boundless energy; I was always amazed how much she accomplished in a short time. She was blessed with a great sense of humor and continually teased and laughed. I always loved to be in her energy field. She was connected to the divine spirit—you could see that in every one of her movements, demeanor, and spoken word. For me my mother was a role model; I often went to her for advice, solace, and perspective. She inspired the concept of a satyagrahi leader—the subject of this book. I am so blessed to have been born to her, as she has been the main architect of shaping my values, morals, and the work I do today in society. Mama, you are very loved and sorely missed, and I hope that this book dedicated to you will be received by you in heaven.

## Lessons Learned from Other Leaders

There is no way to profile all of the leaders who have influenced me in this book. So, in the interest of brevity, I have avoided adding more role models to this book. There are a few more critical leaders who have strongly influenced my views on leadership and life. You can easily research them online for more details about their backgrounds and impacts.

### Marian Wright Edelman

I have known Marian personally since 1996 when she and the Children's Defense Fund (CDF) organized the Stand for Children Rally, which attracted three hundred thousand people from all over the country who gathered at the Mall in Washington, DC. The rally took place in front of the Lincoln Memorial overlooking the Washington Monument, separated by the Reflecting Pool. It was a hot day, and people were seated all the way from the Lincoln Memorial to the Washington Monument, many with their feet in the reflecting pool to cool off. It was an all-day event with many stars and celebrities; they started with one thousand speakers and eventually picked eight. I was fortunate to be one of them and will never forget that day and the energy of three hundred thousand people standing for children. I was interrupted many times with applause in my eight-minute talk. This talk inspired Bob Herbert to write an

Op-Ed piece in the *New York Times*, syndicated nationally to other newspapers, about the rally after hearing my talk as he was walking around the Mall. The piece, entitled "What Unity Looks Like in America," shared my story and complemented CDF's Stand for Children's Rally. Marian is the foremost advocate for children in America and probably in the world. She has been my personal heroine and a role model in terms of what needs to be done for our children. She passionately fights legislation that is not friendly for our children and youth and refuses to take any monies from the US government. We can all learn from this remarkable lady, a brilliant orator and a tireless advocate for children! I am honored to call her a friend. Her ability to honor her values and stay steadfast in her integrity speaks volumes about her competence as a satyagrahi leader.

## Abraham Lincoln

Abraham Lincoln is my favorite president because he came at a perfect time in history to save the Union. As a result, today we are enjoying a nation that is the envy of the world. We are the largest economy, the indisputable super-power, and the wealthiest nation that is a beacon of democracy, meritocracy, freedom, and a land of opportunity. While we do face challenges in many of these areas, I strongly believe in the resilience of the American people. There are many lessons to be learned from this American superhero and statesman. Many are brilliantly narrated in the book *Lincoln on Leadership*, by Donald T. Phillips, a must read for leaders and ones entering the workforce. For me to list all the lessons of Abe would take another book. What has been particularly helpful for me is his ability to assess a situation, not sitting in the ivory tower but engaging with the troops at all levels. He believed in building strong alliances and stayed true to them. One of my favorite quotes attributed to him is, "Do I not destroy my enemies when I make them my friends?" I do relate strongly to this, as much richness and peace has manifested in my life as a result of forgiving my son's killer and befriending him and his grandfather/guardian.

Abe embodied a strong moral fiber, believing that honesty and integrity are the best policies and, importantly, adhering to this always. He only believed in waging one war at a time and only using force as a *last resort*. He was a master of persuasion as opposed to coercion, and with a strong sense of empathy and compassion, he forged many successful relationships. He understood that human action can be modified but human nature cannot be changed. I love that he portrayed hope, which I believe is the essence of what has made America great. He understood that extinguishing hope creates desperation. Abe believed that you must always be fair and decent, both in your professional and personal life. He recognized that any organization will take on the personality of its top leader. One of my favorite lines from his second inaugural address, and a favorite of many others, is to "have malice toward none, with charity for all." He was very careful when it came to expressing anger: under deep duress or distress, which happened often as he was criticized a lot, he would vent his anger by writing harsh letters but never sending them. His humility was becoming, as he gave all the honor and credit to his subordinates when things went right and took the blame when things didn't go so well. A man of vision, a brilliant orator, and an effective communicator—Abraham Lincoln was truly a satyagrahi leader beyond all.

Abe has many amazing leadership qualities, but the two that have helped me the most are his boldness and courageousness. Again, I believe these qualities come from the third competency of our divine nature. So let us all reawaken in ourselves our divine destiny, increasing our awareness of the plight of the other person, igniting our consciences to be bold enough to stand for what is right, what is true, and what is just. The USA and much of the world is very divided today. We have lost the inclusiveness and wisdom of our forefathers like Abe Lincoln and the vision they promulgated to make the USA what it is in a short two hundred forty-three years. It is critical that we reverse this downward spiral, increase the volume of our voices, and work so we can indeed build our country and the world to the vision of great leaders like Abe Lincoln. The question to ask is, "What part am I playing to make this happen?"

## Andrei Sakharov

Andrei Dmitrievich Sakharov was a Russian nuclear physicist, Soviet dissident, and activist for disarmament, peace, and human rights. Renowned as the designer of the Soviet Union's thermonuclear weapons, Sakharov was once a passionate and talented young physicist who believed his work was of vital significance for the balance of power in the world, especially during the tense Cold War. But when the moral implications of his work began to consume him, Sakharov went public with his views, denouncing the weapons and calling for a peaceful coexistence. As a result of his writing and activism, Sakharov was stripped of his job, publicly denounced by the Soviet government, robbed of manuscripts by the KGB, arrested, exiled, and even force-fed during a hunger strike. Despite the ridicule and threats, Sakharov remained a human rights activist until the day he died, earning him the Nobel Peace Prize in 1975 and the International Humanist Award in 1988. Here you see an example of a person who never sacrificed his values and beliefs and lived in concert with the quintessential universal values of a satyagrahi leader. Such adherence and commitment are awe-inspiring.

My lesson from him was that, once he realized the devastating harm of thermonuclear weapons, he had the courage to shift 180 degrees and became an activist for disarmament and human rights. He stayed true on this course despite being beaten, tortured, and ridiculed. It is important to look at one's life and see what activities one is engaged in that do not contribute to the betterment of society and may even be harmful. In the tragedy of my son's death I recognized that I could not promote revenge, division, and hatred, but could instead forgive and unite my community, an important lesson learned from this legendary satyagrahi leader.

# Self, Role Models, and Reflection: Your Turn

While the journey to manifesting one's best in the three competencies (professional, social, spiritual) is lifelong, a one-page summary about you could be a place to start your leadership quest. In completing this page, you are furthering the journey you have already begun to become a satyagrahi leader.

My strengths:

1.

2.

3.

4.

5.

My role models:

1.

2.

3.

4.

5.

6.

7.

8.

9.

10.

The major lesson I have learned from each role model:

Role model #1:

Role model #2:

Role model #3:

Role model #4:

Role model #5:

Role model #6:

Role model #7:

Role model #8:

Role model #9:

Role model #10:

The important questions I need to keep asking myself, inspired by each of my role models, as I journey to become a satyagrahi leader are:

Question #1:

Question #2:

Question #3:

Question #4:

Question #5:

Question #6:

Question #7:

Question #8:

Question #9:

Question #10:

My very best wishes and prayers for your continued forward journey as we all strive to become better satyagrahi leaders, unite in solving many of the tough societal challenges we face, and collectively commit to create a world that works for everyone and one that is at peace. We have had such a world in our history, and we can do it again!

# ACKNOWLEDGMENTS

Bringing this book to completion required help from a host of people, and I give my most heartfelt thanks to:

my late son, Tariq, whose tragic passing inspired a new trajectory of my life of service;

my daughter, Tasreen, who dedicatedly joined me in this new journey of service by leading the Tariq Khamis Foundation;

my grandchildren, Shahin, Khalil, and Miya, who bring much meaning and purpose to my life;

Tariq's mother, Almas, for having given birth and raised Tariq;

my sister, Neyleen, who was the caregiver for both my father and mother and my foundational support after the loss of my mother;

my brother, Nazir, his wife, Shelina, and daughter, Soraiya, for their continued love and support;

the dedicated board and staff of the Tariq Khamisa Foundation, who unselfishly give of their time, treasure, and talent;

and the many thousands of donors and supporters of the Tariq Khamisa Foundation, now in its twenty-fifth year of serving children and youth.

In particular for the creation of this book, I want to thank my good friend of many years Elena Salsitz, who helped me in introducing two of her outstanding students, who helped with research, writing, and editing:

first, to Michaela Wilbanks, affectionately known as Mickey—a million thanks to you for your exceptional contribution to this book from the onset;

second, to Harrison Baum for helping me with the continuation of the research, writing, and editing of the book once Mickey found her full-time position.

I'd also like to thank:

Jessica Shryack, an intelligent and inspirational presenter. She is also an accomplished writer who spearheaded the editing of this book. Her ideas and edits have measurably improved the readability and content of my book.

my good friend Dianne McKay, a dedicated volunteer for Tariq Khamisa Foundation who has served as board secretary for over twenty years and a brilliant proofreader—a million thanks to Dianne for reading the manuscript a few times and for her suggestions.

my good friend Kelly Mellos, a talented artist, author and presenter, for her wise counsel and inputs to the manuscript and for introducing me to Devon Glenn.

Finally, to a brilliant editor, writer, and researcher Devon Glenn, who substantially enhanced the content and readability of my book.

Others I would like to thank include:

Susan Greene, my bookkeeper of many years who helps with many other tasks, including this book, and does it always with passion and a smile.

Noreen O'Sullivan for her continued and dedicated support of my work, books, website, and speaking engagements.

Michelle Rene Buysse, who manages my social media, edits, and disseminates my monthly newsletters, manages and updates my website, and does so with soulful passion.

graphic designer Ken Fraser for the brilliant design of the cover and back cover of this book.

A million thanks to the many who read the manuscript and provided heartfelt endorsement of my fifth book: *Leadership for the Greater Good—A Guide for Truth to Power Champions.* This has truly been a labor of love for all who helped create the final product.

Last, but never the least, to my good friend of many decades and publisher, Bill Gladstone of Waterside Productions, Inc., who provided valuable guidance, and for his continued friendship and support of my writing and work.

Made in the USA
Monee, IL
16 November 2021